Pillsbury

D0443342

SSF

TO

he ea
refr

S.S.F. Public Library
West Orange
840 West Orange Ave.
South San Francisco, CA 94080

JUL   2008

WILEY

ublishing, Inc.

This book is printed on acid-free paper. ∞

Copyright © 2008 by General Mills, Minneapolis, Minnesota. All rights reserved.

Published by John Wiley & Sons, Inc., Hoboken, New Jersey

Published simultaneously in Canada

No part of this publication may be reproduced, stored in a retrieval system, or transmitted in any form or by any means, electronic, mechanical, photocopying, recording, scanning, or otherwise, except as permitted under Section 107 or 108 of the 1976 United States Copyright Act, without either the prior written permission of the Publisher, or authorization through payment of the appropriate per-copy fee to the Copyright Clearance Center, Inc., 222 Rosewood Drive, Danvers, MA 01923, (978) 750-8400, fax (978) 750-4470, or on the web at www.copyright.com. Requests to the Publisher for permission should be addressed to the Permissions Department, John Wiley & Sons, Inc., 111 River Street, Hoboken, NJ 07030, (201) 748-6011, fax (201) 748-6008, or online at http://www.wiley.com/go/permissions.

Trademarks: Wiley and the Wiley Publishing logo are trademarks or registered trademarks of John Wiley & Sons and/or its affiliates. All other trademarks referred to herein are trademarks of General Mills. Wiley Publishing, Inc., is not associated with any product or vendor mentioned in this book.

Limit of Liability/Disclaimer of Warranty: While the publisher and author have used their best efforts in preparing this book, they make no representations or warranties with respect to the accuracy or completeness of the contents of this book and specifically disclaim any implied warranties of merchantability or fitness for a particular purpose. No warranty may be created or extended by sales representatives or written sales materials. The advice and strategies contained herein may not be suitable for your situation. You should consult with a professional where appropriate. Neither the publisher nor author shall be liable for any loss of profit or any other commercial damages, including but not limited to special, incidental, consequential, or other damages.

For general information on our other products and services or for technical support, please contact our Customer Care Department within the United States at (800) 762-2974, outside the United States at (317) 572-3993 or fax (317) 572-4002.

Wiley also publishes its books in a variety of electronic formats. Some content that appears in print may not be available in electronic books. For more information about Wiley products, visit our web site at www.wiley.com.

Library of Congress Cataloging-in-Publication Data:

Pillsbury pizza night : top it, stuff it, twist it—the easy way to go with refrigerated dough / Pillsbury editors.
    p. cm.
  Includes index.
  ISBN 978-0-470-23022-0 (cloth)
  1. Pizza. I. Pillsbury Company.
  TX770.P58.P592 2008
  641.8'248—dc22

                                                              2007039337

General Mills

Publisher, Cookbooks: Maggie Gilbert/Lynn Vettel

Manager and Editor, Cookbooks: Lois Tlusty

Food Editor: Lola Whalen

Recipe Development and Testing: Pillsbury Kitchens

Photography and Food Styling: General Mills Photography Studios and Image Library

Cover Photographer: Carmen Bonilla

Cover Food Stylist: Regina Murphy

For more great recipes visit pillsbury.com

Wiley Publishing, Inc.

Publisher: Natalie Chapman

Executive Editor: Anne Ficklen

Editor: Adam Kowit

Production Manager: Leslie Anglin

Cover Design: Suzanne Sunwoo

Art Director: Tai Blanche

Interior Design and Layout: Tai Blanche and Indianapolis Composition Services

Photography Art Direction: Brent Bentrott

Prop Stylist: Michele Joy

Manufacturing Manager: Kevin Watt

Manufactured in China

10 9 8 7 6 5 4 3 2 1

Cover photo: Personalized Individual Pizzas (page 52)

Welcome...

From the Pillsbury Kitchens

Home of the Pillsbury Bake-Off® Contest

Everyone loves pizza!

And you can make great homemade pizza with the help of refrigerated dough.

It takes minutes to unroll the refrigerated pizza crust, top it with your favorite pizza toppings and pop it in the oven. Nothing says loving like a hot pizza that was created in your kitchen.

Hey, everyone wants to create their own pizza sensation, which means you won't be stuck in the kitchen alone. Let the kids pitch in and help prepare the toppings and load them on the pizza crust. And this one-dish wonder cuts way down on the cleanup because you need only one pan and a few kitchen tools to get the job done.

Watch the kids' faces light up when you present a cookie pizza made easy with refrigerated cookie dough. Or have friends over for pizza and wow them with a creation that they will think you ordered from a restaurant.

Pizza time is anytime and homemade pizza can't be beat!

Warmly,

The Pillsbury Editors

TOC

table of contents

Pizza Pointers

The pizza is sticking to the pan again! The center of the pizza never seems to get done!

Here are some easy tips to help you make homemade pizza better than the local pizzeria.

Handling the Dough

- Spray the pan with cooking spray or brush the pan with olive oil to help prevent the baked pizza from sticking to the pan.
- Dust the pan with cornmeal or flour before pressing the dough in the pan to prevent the baked pizza from sticking to the pan.
- Dip your fingertips into flour before pressing the dough in the pan to prevent the dough from sticking to your fingers.
- Press out the dough from the center to the edge so the edge is slightly thicker than the center to hold in the toppings.

Know Your Crust

For a Thinner/Crispier Crust:

- Dust the pan with cornmeal or flour before pressing the dough in the pan for a crispier crust.
- Press out the dough to about ¼-inch thickness.
- Brush the unbaked dough with olive oil for a crispier, more flavorful crust.

For a Thicker/Traditional Crust:

- Press out the dough to about ½-inch thickness for a softer, chewier crust.

For an Extra Thick/Deep Dish Crust:

- Unroll the dough and place it in a 13×9-inch baking pan. Starting at the center, press out the dough to the edges of the pan and at least 1 inch up sides.

Oven Advice

- Move the oven rack to lowest position.
- Preheat the oven 10 minutes before placing the pizza in the oven.

Topping Tips

- Arrange the toppings and cheese so the center has less than the outer edges. This prevents the center from being undercooked and the edges from being overcooked.
- Keep things simple—more isn't always better. Too much sauce and cheese will tend to pull the cheese and other toppings toward the center of the pizza. This results in an undercooked pizza crust.
- Mozzarella cheese is a great choice because it melts easily and makes those great "cheese strings" when you bite into the pizza. The convenient shredded pizza-cheese blends are also tasty and add more flavor to the pizza.
- Hard cheeses such as shredded or grated Parmesan, Asiago or Romano add flavor and a bit of saltiness to the pizza.
- Semisoft shredded or sliced cheeses, such as provolone, Monterey Jack, Havarti and Colby, melt nicely and add a creamy, rich flavor.
- Add a flavor punch to the pizza by using crumbled blue, Gorgonzola, Roquefort or Stilton cheese.
- Cubes or slices of Brie, Camembert, chèvre (goat) cheese or fresh mozzarella add a rich delicate flavor.

Before the First Bite

- Allow the pizza to cool 2 to 3 minutes before cutting. This allows the cheese to set and makes the pizza easier to cut.
- Use a pizza wheel to cut the pizza into wedges. Start in the center and cut to the edge. This helps prevent pulling the toppings off the wedges.
- You can slip the pizza from the pan onto a cutting board. Use a long sharp knife, such as a chef's knife, and cut the pizza into wedges or squares. Place the knife across the pizza and push down on the tip of the knife and on the handle, and cut with a rocking motion.
- Allow the pizza to cool a few more minutes before taking the first bite because hot cheese can easily burn your mouth. If you do accidentally burn your mouth, immediately put an ice cube in your mouth to help stop the burning and prevent blistering. Or drink a glass of milk to help prevent further burning.

Refrigerated Pizza Crust

Q&A

Who doesn't love the convenience of refrigerated pizza crust to make hot-out-of-the-oven homemade pizza to delight family and friends? Here are answers to some of the most frequently asked questions about using refrigerated pizza crust.

Q: How long can I store unopened cans of refrigerated pizza crust?
A: For best quality, use refrigerated dough before the "use-by" date on the package.

Q: Where should I store the dough?
A: Store dough cans on a shelf in the refrigerator. Temperatures in the refrigerator's door shelves may be too warm, and the crisper may be too cold. Keep dough refrigerated until just before baking. Warm dough may be sticky and hard to handle.

Q: What if I forget to refrigerate the dough?
A: Cans of dough that are left unrefrigerated for more than two hours should be discarded.

Q: Can I use some of the dough now and save some for later?
A: Opening the can of dough activates the leavening that causes the dough to rise. After the can is open, the dough can be covered with plastic wrap and refrigerated for up to two hours before baking. After two hours, the dough will begin to deteriorate.

Q: Can I freeze the unbaked dough?
A: No. Freezing unbaked dough may prevent it from rising once it is baked.

Q: Can I freeze the baked crust?
A: Yes, you can freeze the baked crust. For best results, use within one month after freezing.

Q: Can I microwave the unbaked dough?
A: No. The uneven heat of a microwave prevents the dough from baking evenly, and the crust won't brown.

Q: Can I bake refrigerated dough in a toaster oven?
A: No, it is not recommended. A toaster oven's small size often results in uneven heating, and the crust may burn.

Q: Do I need to preheat the oven?
A: Yes, preheat the oven for 10 minutes before baking. This important step will help prevent the pizza from baking unevenly.

Q: Do I need to prebake the crust before adding the toppings?
A: It is not necessary to prebake the crust. However, prebaking will result in a crispier crust. Preheat the oven to 400°F and bake the untopped dough for 7 minutes. Top with toppings. Bake at 400°F for 6 to 11 minutes more.

Q: Can the pizza crust be baked on a baking stone or pizza stone?
A: It depends on the type of stone. We do not recommend using a pizza or baking stone that requires preheating before the assembled pizza is placed on it. The unbaked crust is too soft to lift once the toppings have been added. Pizza crust may be baked on a stone that does not require preheating. Follow the directions that came with the stone for baking time and temperature.

QUICK PIZZA CRUST IDEAS

Easy Stromboli

1 Heat oven to 400°F. Unroll refrigerated pizza crust dough; place on greased cookie sheet. Press dough into a 12x8-inch rectangle.

2 Spread ¼ cup pizza sauce on dough to within 2 inches of long sides, and sprinkle with ½ red or green pepper (if desired), 1 cup shredded cheese and ¼ teaspoon dried Italian seasoning. Fold long sides of dough over filling; pinch to seal. Pinch short sides to seal.

3 Bake 15 to 20 minutes or until crust is golden brown.

Stuffed-Crust Pizza

1 Heat oven to 425°F. Unroll refrigerated pizza crust dough and press in bottom and 1 inch up the sides of a greased 13x9-inch pan.

2 Place seven sticks of string cheese along the inside edges of the dough. Fold dough around the cheese; press to seal. Top with desired ingredients.

3 Bake 15 to 18 minutes or until crust is golden brown and cheese is melted.

Pizza + Family = Fun

Gather the family together and try some of these fun pizza occasions. It won't be long before your kids will be initiating their own occasions to eat pizza!

BOARD-GAME NIGHT

Make a checkerboard pizza to kick off family board-game night. Unroll a refrigerated pizza crust on a baking sheet. Let the kids spread the pizza sauce across the crust. Then alternate squares of cheese with slices of pepperoni in a checkerboard pattern all across the pizza crust.

AFTER-SCHOOL DIPPIN'

Have the refrigerated pizza crust unrolled and ready to make an after-school snack when the kids walk in the door. Cut the dough into 1-inch squares using a pizza cutter. Let the kids brush the squares with Italian or ranch dressing and sprinkle with shredded Parmesan cheese and some dried herbs. Bake. Then the kids can dip them in pizza or pasta tomato sauce that has been warmed in the microwave.

HOMEWORK HELPER

Have a pizza incentive to help get the kids motivated to do their homework. The kids can top an unrolled refrigerated pizza crust with their favorite toppings. Pop it in the oven and start the homework. When the pizza's done, they'll have taken a big bite out of their homework and can celebrate with a piece of pizza.

PIZZA PICNIC

On days when it's too cold or wet to be outdoors, have an indoor picnic. Unroll a refrigerated pizza crust and create a family-pleasin' pizza. While it bakes in the oven, spread a sheet on the floor, gather paper plates and napkins and some beverages. When the pizza is done, it's picnic time—indoors.

SLEEPOVER TREAT

Create a late-night snack and capture the creativity of the sleepy-headed overnight guests. Have a variety of pizza toppings to create funny-face pizzas. Cut circles of refrigerated pizza crust dough with a round cutter about 4 inches across (a clean empty can works well for this). Spread each circle with pizza sauce and have each kid create their own pizza face. Try shredded cheese for the hair, a half-pepperoni slice for the mouth, olives for the eyes and a strip of bell pepper for the nose.

FAMILY MOVIE NIGHT

Nothing beats an evening at home watching movies together. Start the evening with creating your own individual pizzas. Unroll refrigerated pizza crust and cut each crust into four pieces. Give each family member a square or two of dough so everyone can create a personalized pizza. Set out a large bowl of tossed salad with bottles of salad dressings. While the pizzas bake, select the movie lineup for the evening.

REFRIGERATOR PIZZA NIGHT

If it's been a busy week and there was no time for grocery shopping, unroll the refrigerated pizza crust you keep on hand and spread it with pizza sauce. Let everyone select one or two items from the refrigerator to put on top of the pizza. (Or check out Family Movie Night and make individual pizzas.) Select beverages from the refrigerator and fruit for dessert for an easy, relaxing dinner.

1

Pizza for Family Meals

California Pizzas

Prep Time: **15 Minutes**   Start to Finish: **30 Minutes**   2 pizzas

2 Pillsbury Grands!® frozen buttermilk biscuits (from 16-oz bag)

2 teaspoons Italian dressing

1 medium plum (Roma) tomato, sliced

4 fresh basil leaves, sliced

¼ cup frozen diced cooked chicken breast (from 9-oz package)

¼ cup shredded Italian cheese blend (1 oz)

1 Heat oven to 400°F. To thaw biscuits, place on microwavable plate; microwave uncovered on High 15 to 30 seconds or until biscuits are soft enough to press into rounds.

2 Place biscuits on ungreased cookie sheet. Press or roll each to form 6-inch round. Spread 1 teaspoon dressing on each round. Top each evenly with remaining ingredients.

3 Bake 13 to 15 minutes or until crust is golden brown and cheese is melted.

1 Pizza: Calories 300; Total Fat 15g (Saturated Fat 5g; Trans Fat 4g); Cholesterol 35mg; Sodium 960mg; Total Carbohydrate 26g (Dietary Fiber 0g) • **Exchanges:** 1 ½ Starch, 1 ½ Lean Meat, 2 Fat • **Carbohydrate Choices:** 2

pizza bites Fresh basil is very perishable. Process leftover leaves in a food processor with a little olive oil. Freeze small dollops on a small cookie sheet. Remove and seal in a freezer bag. Use one or two to flavor other dishes such as casseroles, spaghetti or soups.

Easy Breakfast Pizza

Bake-Off® Contest 38, 1998   Ernest Crow   Rockville, MD

Prep Time: **15 Minutes**   Start to Finish: **30 Minutes**   8 servings

1 can (13.8 oz) Pillsbury refrigerated classic pizza crust	2 tablespoons butter or margarine
8 eggs	1 container (8 oz) chives-and-onion, garden vegetable or regular cream cheese spread
¼ cup half-and-half or milk	
⅛ teaspoon salt	8 slices crisply cooked bacon
⅛ teaspoon pepper	Chopped green onions, if desired

1 Heat oven to 425°F. Grease 12-inch pizza pan with shortening or spray with cooking spray. Unroll dough; place in pan. Starting at center, press out dough to edge of pan.

2 Meanwhile, in medium bowl, beat eggs, half-and-half, salt and pepper with wire whisk until well blended. In 10-inch skillet, melt butter over medium heat. Add egg mixture; cook, stirring occasionally, until thoroughly cooked but still moist. Remove from heat.

3 Spoon cooked egg mixture over dough. Drop cream cheese spread by teaspoonfuls over eggs. Arrange bacon in spoke fashion on top of pizza.

4 Bake 12 to 15 minutes longer or until crust is deep golden brown and toppings are hot. Garnish with onions.

1 Serving: Calories 360; Total Fat 22g (Saturated Fat 11g; Trans Fat 0g); Cholesterol 255mg; Sodium 850mg; Total Carbohydrate 25g (Dietary Fiber 0g) • **Exchanges:** 1 ½ Starch, 1 ½ High-Fat Meat, 2 Fat • **Carbohydrate Choices:** 1 ½

pizza bites This is great for a weekend breakfast but also makes a tasty weeknight supper. For a crispier crust, bake crust 6 to 7 minutes or until crust just begins to brown, then add toppings; bake pizza 8 to 12 minutes longer.

Denver Scrambled Egg Pizza

Prep Time: **25 Minutes**   Start to Finish: **25 Minutes**   4 pizzas

1 can (13.8 oz) Pillsbury refrigerated classic pizza crust

1 tablespoon butter or margarine

1 cup frozen bell pepper and onion stir-fry (from 1-lb bag)

8 eggs

2 tablespoons milk

¼ teaspoon salt

½ cup chopped cooked ham

2 to 3 tablespoons creamy Dijon mustard-mayonnaise spread

1 Heat oven to 400°F. Lightly spray large cookie sheet with cooking spray. Unroll dough on work surface. Cut dough into 4 equal pieces; place on cookie sheet. Starting at center, press out each piece of dough to form 6×5-inch rectangle. With fingers, create slight rim on edge of each dough rectangle. Bake 11 to 15 minutes or until golden brown.

2 Meanwhile, in 12-inch nonstick skillet, melt butter over medium heat. Add bell pepper and onion stir-fry; cook 3 to 5 minutes or until tender, stirring occasionally.

3 In medium bowl, mix eggs, milk, salt and ham; beat well. Add to skillet; cook 4 to 5 minutes or until thoroughly cooked and eggs are set but still moist, stirring occasionally.

4 Spread each baked crust with mustard-mayonnaise spread. Spoon egg mixture evenly over top. Serve warm.

1 Pizza: Calories 470; Total Fat 18g (Saturated Fat 6g; Trans Fat 0g); Cholesterol 440mg; Sodium 1360mg; Total Carbohydrate 53g (Dietary Fiber 0g) • **Exchanges:** 2 ½ Starch, 1 Other Carbohydrate, 2 ½ Medium-Fat Meat, ½ Fat • **Carbohydrate Choices:** 3 ½

pizza bites If you don't have the bell pepper and onion stir-fry in your freezer, use 1/2 cup each chopped fresh bell pepper and onion.

Stuffed-Crust Pizza

Prep Time: **15 Minutes**   Start to Finish: **35 Minutes**   8 servings

1 can (13.8 oz) Pillsbury refrigerated classic pizza crust

7 sticks (1 oz each) string cheese

½ cup pizza sauce

24 slices pepperoni (from 3.5-oz package)

2 cups shredded Italian cheese blend (8 oz)

1 Heat oven to 425°F. Grease 12-inch pizza pan with shortening, or spray with cooking spray. Unroll dough; place in pan. Starting at center, press out dough to edge of pan and at least 1 inch up sides.

2 Place string cheese around inside edge of crust. Fold extended edge of dough over cheese; pinch firmly to seal.

3 Spread sauce evenly over dough. Top with pepperoni and cheese blend.

4 Bake 12 to 16 minutes or until crust is deep golden brown and cheese in center is melted. Cut into wedges.

1 Serving: Calories 370; Total Fat 20g (Saturated Fat 11g; Trans Fat 0g); Cholesterol 60mg; Sodium 1050mg; Total Carbohydrate 27g (Dietary Fiber 0g) • **Exchanges:** 1 ½ Starch, ½ Other Carbohydrate, 2 High-Fat Meat, ½ Fat • **Carbohydrate Choices:** 2

pizza bites Smoked string cheese can be used instead of the regular string cheese. And, if you don't have pizza sauce on hand, you can use tomato pasta sauce or salsa.

Double-Crust Pizza Supreme

Prep Time: **25 Minutes**   Start to Finish: **1 Hour 5 Minutes**   8 servings

1 package (12 oz) bulk pork sausage

2 cans (13.8 oz each) Pillsbury refrigerated pizza crust

1 package (3.5 oz) pepperoni slices

1 jar (14 oz) pizza sauce

1 jar (4.5 oz) sliced mushrooms, drained

1 medium green bell pepper, cut into ¼-inch-thick rings, if desired

1 medium onion, chopped (½ cup), if desired

8 slices (¾ oz each) mozzarella cheese

2 tablespoons grated Parmesan cheese

1   Heat oven to 375°F. Lightly spray 12-inch pizza pan with cooking spray.

2   Meanwhile, in 10-inch skillet, cook sausage over medium heat, stirring frequently, until no longer pink; drain well on paper towels. Unroll 1 can of dough; place on pizza pan. Starting at center, press out dough to edge of pan. Layer sausage and pepperoni on dough. With back of spoon, carefully spread 1/2 cup of the pizza sauce evenly over pepperoni. Top with mushrooms, bell pepper, onion and slices of mozzarella cheese.

3   Unroll remaining can of dough; place on work surface. Starting at center, press out dough into 12-inch round. Fold dough in half; place over mozzarella cheese, and unfold. Press edge to seal. Cut several slits in top crust for steam to escape. Sprinkle Parmesan cheese over top.

4   Bake 35 to 40 minutes or until crust is deep golden brown. Meanwhile, in 1-quart saucepan, heat remaining pizza sauce. Cut pizza into wedges; serve topped with warm pizza sauce.

1 Serving: Calories 470; Total Fat 18g (Saturated Fat 8g; Trans Fat 0g); Cholesterol 45mg; Sodium 1500mg; Total Carbohydrate 53g (Dietary Fiber 1g) • **Exchanges:** 2 ½ Starch, 1 Other Carbohydrate, 2 High-Fat Meat • **Carbohydrate Choices:** 3 ½

"Love You" Pizzas

Prep Time: **20 Minutes**   Start to Finish: **30 Minutes**   4 pizzas

1 can (13.8 oz) Pillsbury
  refrigerated classic pizza crust
1 can (8 oz) pizza sauce

24 slices turkey pepperoni
¾ cup shredded mozzarella
  cheese (3 oz)

1 Heat oven to 425°F. Lightly spray large cookie sheet with cooking spray.

2 Unroll dough. Cut dough into 4 equal portions. Place on cookie sheet. Cut 1-inch slit in center of wide edge of each dough portion; on opposite wide edge across from slit, pinch dough together to shape point of heart. Slightly separate each cut slit and gently press dough into a 6×5-inch heart, creating slight rim on edge of dough.

3 Bake for 5 minutes or until crusts are light golden brown.

4 Divide pizza sauce evenly onto partially baked crusts, spreading to within 1/2 inch of edges. Top each with 6 slices pepperoni and scant 3 tablespoons cheese.

5 Bake 7 to 9 minutes longer or until crust edges are golden brown and cheese is melted.

1 Pizza: Calories 400; Total Fat 12g (Saturated Fat 4.5g; Trans Fat 0g); Cholesterol 40mg; Sodium 1670mg; Total Carbohydrate 52g (Dietary Fiber 0g) • **Exchanges:** 2 ½ Starch, 1 Other Carbohydrate, 2 Lean Meat, 1 Fat • **Carbohydrate Choices:** 3 ½

pizza bites Let your family know you love them with personalized heart-shaped pizzas. Have each family member top their pizza with their favorite toppings. Try sliced ripe olives and mushrooms, chopped onions, diced green bell pepper, pineapple chunks and shredded Cheddar cheese.

Pepperoni Pizza with Tomatoes

Prep Time: **10 Minutes**   Start to Finish: **30 Minutes**   4 servings

1 can (13.8 oz) Pillsbury
  refrigerated classic pizza crust

1 can (8 oz) pizza sauce

½ cup sliced pepperoni

2 medium plum (Roma)
  tomatoes, seeded, chopped

1 cup shredded mozzarella
  cheese (4 oz)

1 tablespoon grated Parmesan
  cheese

1   Move oven rack to lowest position. Heat oven to 425°F. Spray 15×10-inch pan with cooking spray. Unroll dough; place in pan. Starting at center, press out dough to edges of pan.

2   Spread pizza sauce over crust to within 1/2 inch of edges. Top with pepperoni, tomatoes and mozzarella cheese. Sprinkle with Parmesan cheese.

3   Bake 14 to 18 minutes or until crust is golden brown.

1 Serving: Calories 420; Total Fat 14g (Saturated Fat 7g; Trans Fat 0g); Cholesterol 30mg; Sodium 1360mg; Total Carbohydrate 54g (Dietary Fiber 1g) • **Exchanges:** 2 ½ Starch, 1 Other Carbohydrate, 1 ½ High-Fat Meat • **Carbohydrate Choices:** 3 ½

Chicken and Black Bean Tostizzas

Bake-Off® Contest 36, 1994   Karen Durrett   Portland, OR

Prep Time: **15 Minutes**   Start to Finish: **40 Minutes**   8 servings

1 can (16.3 oz) Pillsbury Grands! Flaky Layers refrigerated original biscuits

1 cup diced cooked chicken

1 cup black beans (from 15-oz can), drained

½ cup chunky-style salsa

¼ cup chopped fresh cilantro

¼ teaspoon ground cumin

2 medium green onions, chopped (2 tablespoons)

½ cup green or red bell pepper strips (1 inch long)

1 ½ cups shredded Cheddar cheese (6 oz)

½ cup sour cream, if desired

½ cup guacamole, if desired

1 Heat oven to 350°F. Separate dough into 8 biscuits. On ungreased cookie sheets, press or roll each to form 5 1/2-inch rounds.

2 In medium bowl, mix chicken, black beans, salsa, cilantro and cumin. Spread evenly over biscuits to within 1/4 inch of edges. Top evenly with onions, bell pepper strips and cheese.

3 Bake 20 to 24 minutes or until biscuits are golden brown and cheese is melted. Garnish with sour cream and guacamole.

1 Serving: Calories 350; Total Fat 17g (Saturated Fat 7g; Trans Fat 3.5g); Cholesterol 35mg; Sodium 880mg; Total Carbohydrate 31g (Dietary Fiber 2g) • **Exchanges:** 1 ½ Starch, ½ Other Carbohydrate, 1 ½ Medium-Fat Meat, 2 Fat • **Carbohydrate Choices:** 2

pizza bites Diced or shredded cooked beef or pork can be used for the chicken.

Easy Sausage-Cheese Pizza

Prep Time: **20 Minutes**   Start to Finish: **35 Minutes**   8 servings

1 can (13.8 oz) Pillsbury refrigerated classic pizza crust

½ lb bulk light turkey and pork sausage

1 can (14.5 oz) stewed tomatoes, drained

½ teaspoon dried oregano leaves

⅛ teaspoon crushed red pepper flakes

1 clove garlic, finely chopped or ⅛ teaspoon garlic powder

2 tablespoons grated Parmesan cheese

2 cups shredded mozzarella cheese (8 oz)

1 Heat oven to 425°F. Spray 13×9-inch pan with cooking spray. Unroll dough; place in pan. Starting at center, press out dough to edges of pan and 1/2 inch up sides. Bake 7 minutes.

2 Meanwhile, in 8-inch skillet, cook sausage over medium-high heat, stirring frequently, until no longer pink. Remove sausage from skillet; drain on paper towels.

3 In same skillet, mix tomatoes, oregano, red pepper and garlic; cook over medium-high heat until bubbly. Reduce heat to medium-low; simmer uncovered 5 to 8 minutes, stirring occasionally, to blend flavors.

4 Spread tomato mixture over partially baked crust. Sprinkle sausage evenly over tomato mixture. Top with Parmesan and mozzarella cheeses.

5 Bake 10 to 12 minutes longer or until crust is golden brown and cheese is melted. Cut into squares.

1 Serving: Calories 280; Total Fat 11g (Saturated Fat 5g; Trans Fat 0g); Cholesterol 45mg; Sodium 870mg; Total Carbohydrate 28g (Dietary Fiber 0g) • **Exchanges:** 1 Starch, 1 Other Carbohydrate, 2 Medium-Fat Meat • **Carbohydrate Choices:** 2

Barbecue Pork and Veggie Pizza

Prep Time: **10 Minutes**   Start to Finish: **25 Minutes**   4 servings

1 can (13.8 oz) Pillsbury refrigerated classic pizza crust

1 container (18 oz) refrigerated original barbecue sauce with shredded pork

1 ½ cups shredded Monterey Jack cheese (6 oz)

½ medium red onion (halved lengthwise), cut into thin wedges

1 medium green bell pepper, cut into thin bite-size strips

1 Heat oven to 425°F. Spray 12-inch pizza pan with cooking spray. Unroll dough; place in pan. Starting at center, press out dough to edge of pan. Bake 7 to 9 minutes or until light golden brown.

2 Spoon barbecue sauce with pork over partially baked crust. Top with cheese, onion and bell pepper.

3 Bake 10 to 12 minutes longer or until crust is golden brown and cheese is melted.

1 Serving: Calories 610; Total Fat 20g (Saturated Fat 10g; Trans Fat 0g); Cholesterol 70mg; Sodium 1790mg; Total Carbohydrate 74g (Dietary Fiber 0g) • **Exchanges:** 3 Starch, 2 Other Carbohydrate, 3 Medium-Fat Meat, ½ Fat • **Carbohydrate Choices:** 5

Chicago Deep-Dish Sausage Pizza

Prep Time: **25 Minutes**   Start to Finish: **50 Minutes**   6 servings

1 lb bulk Italian pork sausage

½ cup chopped green bell pepper

1 cup sliced fresh mushrooms (3 oz)

1 can (8 oz) pizza sauce

1 can (13.8 oz) Pillsbury refrigerated classic pizza crust

1 ½ cups shredded mozzarella cheese (6 oz)

2 medium plum (Roma) tomatoes, chopped

¼ cup sliced ripe olives, if desired

2 tablespoons chopped green onions (2 medium)

1 Heat oven to 400°F. Spray 9-inch square pan with cooking spray. In 10-inch nonstick skillet, cook sausage and bell pepper over medium-high heat 7 to 9 minutes, stirring frequently, until sausage is no longer pink. Stir in mushrooms and pizza sauce. Keep warm over low heat.

2 Unroll dough; place in pan. Starting at center, press out dough to edges of pan, pressing up and at least 1 inch up sides, folding edge under to form crust. Sprinkle 1/2 cup of the cheese evenly in bottom of crust. Spoon hot sausage mixture over cheese. Top with remaining 1 cup cheese, the tomatoes and olives.

3 Bake 15 to 20 minutes or until crust is golden brown. Sprinkle with onions. Let stand 5 minutes before cutting.

1 Serving: Calories 390; Total Fat 18g (Saturated Fat 7g; Trans Fat 0g); Cholesterol 45mg; Sodium 1050mg; Total Carbohydrate 37g (Dietary Fiber 1g) • **Exchanges:** 2 Starch, ½ Other Carbohydrate, 2 High-Fat Meat • **Carbohydrate Choices:** 2 ½

pizza bites Keep refrigerated dough, such as pizza crust dough, chilled in the original package until you are ready to use it. Refrigerated dough is easy to work with when it is very cold.

Rustic Ham and Spinach Pie

Prep Time: **25 Minutes**   Start to Finish: **55 Minutes**   6 servings

1 can (13.8 oz) Pillsbury
refrigerated classic pizza crust

2 teaspoons olive or vegetable
oil

½ teaspoon minced garlic
(½ to 1 clove)

1 box (9 oz) frozen spinach in
pouch, thawed, squeezed to
drain

1 package (8 oz) sliced Swiss
cheese

8 oz thinly sliced cooked ham

1   Heat oven to 425°F. Spray 9-inch round cake pan with cooking spray. Unroll dough; place in pan. Starting at center, press out dough to edge of pan and up sides. Roll top edge under and press against top rim of pan to secure.

2   In small bowl, mix oil and garlic. Brush dough with 1 teaspoon of the oil mixture. Place spinach on bottom of crust; top with half of the cheese. Place ham over cheese; brush with remaining oil mixture. Place remaining cheese on top. Place strips of foil around edge of crust.

3   Bake 25 to 30 minutes or until crust is lightly browned and cheese is melted.

1 Serving: Calories 420; Total Fat 18g (Saturated Fat 9g; Trans Fat 0g); Cholesterol 55mg; Sodium 1180mg; Total Carbohydrate 37g (Dietary Fiber 3g) • **Exchanges:** 2 Starch, ½ Other Carbohydrate, 3 Medium-Fat Meat • **Carbohydrate Choices:** 2 ½

pizza bites For a crispier crust, bake crust 7 to 9 minutes or until light golden brown, then add toppings; bake pizza 20 to 25 minutes longer.

Easy Taco Pizza

Prep Time: **25 Minutes**   Start to Finish: **45 Minutes**   6 servings

1 lb ground beef

½ cup chopped onion

1 can (2 ¼ oz) sliced ripe
olives, drained

1 can (8 oz) tomato sauce

1 envelope (1.25 oz) taco
seasoning mix

1 can (13.8 oz) Pillsbury
refrigerated classic pizza crust

1 cup shredded Cheddar
cheese (4 oz)

Shredded lettuce

Chopped seeded tomato

Sour cream

Sliced avocado

Chopped green onions

1   Heat oven to 425°F. Spray 12-inch pizza pan or 13×9-inch pan with
cooking spray. Unroll dough; place in pan. Starting at center, press
out dough to edge of pan.

2   In 10-inch skillet, cook beef and onion over medium-high heat 5 to
7 minutes, stirring frequently, until thoroughly cooked; drain. Stir in
olives, tomato sauce and taco seasoning mix.

3   Spread ground beef mixture over crust; sprinkle with cheese.

4   Bake 15 to 20 minutes or until crust is golden brown. Top with lettuce,
tomato, sour cream, avocado and onions.

1 Serving: Calories 420; Total Fat 18g (Saturated Fat 8g; Trans Fat 0.5g); Cholesterol
65mg; Sodium 1140mg; Total Carbohydrate 40g (Dietary Fiber 1g) • **Exchanges:** 1 ½
Starch, 1 Other Carbohydrate, 2 ½ Medium-Fat Meat, 1 Fat • **Carbohydrate Choices:** 2 ½

Wild West Pizza

Prep Time: **20 Minutes**   Start to Finish: **35 Minutes**   6 servings

1 can (13.8 oz) Pillsbury refrigerated classic pizza crust

½ lb lean (at least 80%) ground beef

¼ teaspoon salt

⅛ teaspoon pepper

1 can (16 oz) refried beans

1 cup taco sauce or chunky-style salsa

1 can (11 oz) whole kernel corn with red and green peppers, well drained

1 cup shredded Cheddar cheese (4 oz)

2 cups shredded lettuce

1 medium tomato, chopped (¾ cup)

½ cup sliced green onions (8 medium), if desired

1 Heat oven to 400°F. Spray large cookie sheet or 14-inch pizza pan with cooking spray. Unroll dough; place on cookie sheet or in pan. Starting at center, press out dough into 14×12-inch rectangle or to edge of pizza pan. Bake 8 to 10 minutes or until edges of crust begin to brown.

2 Meanwhile, in 8-inch skillet, cook ground beef sprinkled with salt and pepper over medium-high heat, stirring frequently, until thoroughly cooked; drain.

3 Spread refried beans evenly over partially baked crust. Spread 1/2 cup of the taco sauce over beans. Top with ground beef mixture, corn and cheese.

4 Bake 10 to 14 minutes longer or until crust is golden brown and cheese is melted. Top with lettuce, tomatoes and onions. Cut into squares or wedges; serve with remaining 1/2 cup taco sauce.

1 Serving: Calories 440; Total Fat 14g (Saturated Fat 6g; Trans Fat 0g); Cholesterol 50mg; Sodium 1360mg; Total Carbohydrate 56g (Dietary Fiber 6g) • **Exchanges:** 2 ½ Starch, 1 Other Carbohydrate, 2 Medium-Fat Meat, ½ Fat • **Carbohydrate Choices:** 4

pizza bites If you like green chiles, add a 4.5-ounce can of chopped green chiles to the cooked ground beef mixture.

Sloppy Joe Pizza

Prep Time: **20 Minutes**   Start to Finish: **45 Minutes**   8 servings

1 lb lean (at least 80%) ground beef

1 can (15.5 oz) sloppy joe sauce

Cornmeal

1 can (13.8 oz) Pillsbury refrigerated classic pizza crust

¼ cup sliced green onions (4 medium)

1 cup shredded Cheddar cheese (4 oz)

1 Heat oven to 425°F. In 10-inch skillet, cook beef over medium-high heat 5 to 7 minutes, stirring occasionally, until thoroughly cooked; drain. Stir in sloppy joe sauce. Reduce heat; simmer uncovered 5 minutes.

2 Meanwhile, sprinkle cornmeal on 14-inch pizza stone. Unroll dough; place on pizza stone. Starting at center, press out dough into 14-inch round, forming 1/2-inch rim.

3 Spoon hot beef mixture over dough. Top with onions and cheese.

4 Bake 18 to 23 minutes or until crust is golden brown.

1 Serving: Calories 300; Total Fat 13g (Saturated Fat 6g; Trans Fat 0.5g); Cholesterol 50mg; Sodium 790mg; Total Carbohydrate 30g (Dietary Fiber 0g) • **Exchanges:** 1 ½ Starch, ½ Other Carbohydrate, 2 Medium-Fat Meat • **Carbohydrate Choices:** 2

Easy Cheeseburger Pizza

Prep Time: **15 Minutes**   Start to Finish: **35 Minutes**   4 servings

1 can (13.8 oz) Pillsbury
  refrigerated classic pizza crust

½ lb extra-lean (at least 90%)
  ground beef

1 cup tomato pasta sauce

¼ cup chopped red onion,
  if desired

1 cup shredded Cheddar
  cheese (4 oz)

¼ cup dill pickle slices

1 Heat oven to 425°F. Spray 12-inch pizza pan with cooking spray. Unroll dough; place in pan. Starting at center, press out dough to edge of pan, forming 1/2-inch rim. Bake 7 to 9 minutes or until light golden brown.

2 Meanwhile, in 8-inch skillet, cook ground beef over medium-high heat, stirring frequently, until thoroughly cooked; drain.

3 Spread pasta sauce evenly over partially baked crust. Top with cooked ground beef, onion and cheese.

4 Bake 12 to 18 minutes longer or until topping is bubbly and edges are golden brown. Top with pickle slices before serving.

1 Serving: Calories 510; Total Fat 19g (Saturated Fat 9g; Trans Fat 0.5g); Cholesterol 65mg; Sodium 1340mg; Total Carbohydrate 59g (Dietary Fiber 1g) • **Exchanges:** 2 ½ Starch, 1 ½ Other Carbohydrate, 2 ½ Medium-Fat Meat, 1 Fat • **Carbohydrate Choices:** 4

pizza bites For a crispier crust, omit spraying the pizza pan and, instead, sprinkle it with cornmeal before unrolling the dough.

Buffalo Chicken Pizzas

Bake-Off® Contest 39, 2000   Kristin McLaughlin   Boyertown, PA

Prep Time: **20 Minutes**   Start to Finish: **40 Minutes**   4 pizzas

Olive oil

1 can (13.8 oz) Pillsbury refrigerated classic pizza crust

3 tablespoons butter or margarine

1 lb boneless skinless chicken breasts, cut into ½-inch pieces

1 medium sweet onion, chopped (½ cup)

3 tablespoons red pepper sauce

3 plum (Roma) tomatoes, diced (1 cup)

1 cup shredded Monterey Jack cheese (4 oz)

1 Heat oven to 425°F. Lightly coat cookie sheet with olive oil. Unroll dough; with sharp knife or pizza cutter, cut into 4 rectangles. Place rectangles on cookie sheet; press each into 6×5-inch rectangle.

2 In 10-inch skillet, melt butter over medium-high heat. Add chicken, onion and pepper sauce; cook 4 to 6 minutes, stirring occasionally, until chicken is no longer pink in center. Remove from heat; stir in tomatoes.

3 With slotted spoon, spoon mixture over dough rectangles to within 1/4 inch of edges. Sprinkle evenly with cheese.

4 Bake 13 to 16 minutes or until crust is deep golden brown.

1 Pizza: Calories 590; Total Fat 25g (Saturated Fat 13g; Trans Fat 0.5g); Cholesterol 115mg; Sodium 1050mg; Total Carbohydrate 51g (Dietary Fiber 1g) • **Exchanges:** 2 ½ Starch, 1 Other Carbohydrate, 4 ½ Lean Meat, 2 Fat • **Carbohydrate Choices:** 3 ½

5-Way Cincinnati Pizza

Bake-Off® Contest 40, 2002   Melody Levault   Mulkeytown, IL

Prep Time: **15 Minutes**   Start to Finish: **30 Minutes**   6 servings

---

1 can (13.8 oz) Pillsbury refrigerated classic pizza crust

½ lb lean (at least 80%) ground beef

½ cup barbecue sauce

1 to 2 teaspoons chili powder

½ teaspoon salt

½ teaspoon ground cumin

½ teaspoon apple pie spice

1 can (15 or 15.5 oz) red kidney beans, drained, rinsed

1 medium onion, chopped (½ cup)

2 cups shredded Cheddar cheese (8 oz)

---

1 Heat oven to 425°F. Spray 12-inch pizza pan or 13×9-inch pan with cooking spray. Unroll dough; place in pan. Starting at center, press out dough to edge of pan. Bake 7 to 10 minutes or until light golden brown.

2 Meanwhile, in 12-inch skillet, cook ground beef over medium-high heat, stirring frequently, until thoroughly cooked; drain. Stir in barbecue sauce, chili powder, salt, cumin and apple pie spice. Cook 1 minute, stirring constantly.

3 Spread ground beef mixture over partially baked crust. Top with beans, onion and cheese.

4 Bake 11 to 14 minutes longer or until crust is deep golden brown.

---

1 Serving: Calories 500; Total Fat 19g (Saturated Fat 10g; Trans Fat 0.5g); Cholesterol 65mg; Sodium 1140mg; Total Carbohydrate 56g (Dietary Fiber 4g) • **Exchanges:** 2 ½ Starch, 1 Other Carbohydrate, 2 ½ Medium-Fat Meat, 1 Fat • **Carbohydrate Choices:** 4

pizza bites This pizza gets its roots from the famous chili served in Cincinnati. You may be surprised by the apple pie spice ingredient, but it's not a mistake—it adds a nice flavor to the pizza!

Easy Mexican Chicken Pizza

Prep Time: **15 Minutes**   Start to Finish: **30 Minutes**   4 servings

1 can (13.8 oz) Pillsbury refrigerated classic pizza crust

1 cup refried beans (from 6-oz can), stirred

½ cup chunky-style salsa

1½ cups shredded hot pepper Monterey Jack cheese (6 oz)

1 package (6 oz) refrigerated cooked southwestern-flavored chicken breast strips

¼ cup diced plum (Roma) tomato

1   Heat oven to 425°F. Spray 12- or 14-inch pizza pan with cooking spray. Unroll dough; place in pan. Starting at center, press out dough to form 12-inch round. Bake about 8 minutes or until crust begins to brown.

2   Spread refried beans evenly over partially baked crust. Spread salsa over beans. Sprinkle with cheese, chicken and tomato.

3   Bake 9 to 12 minutes longer or until edges of crust are golden brown and cheese is melted. Cut into wedges to serve.

1 Serving: Calories 500; Total Fat 16g (Saturated Fat 8g; Trans Fat 0g); Cholesterol 65mg; Sodium 1600mg; Total Carbohydrate 61g (Dietary Fiber 4g) • **Exchanges:** 3 Starch, 1 Other Carbohydrate, 3 Lean Meat, 1 Fat • **Carbohydrate Choices:** 4

pizza bites   Try your favorite shredded cheese, such as Cheddar or Mexican blend, in place of hot pepper Monterey Jack cheese.

Hearty Reuben Pizza

Bake-Off® Contest 34, 1990   Marie Mickelson   Columbia Heights, MN

Prep Time: **20 Minutes**   Start to Finish: **30 Minutes**   8 servings

1 can (13.8 oz) Pillsbury refrigerated classic pizza crust	2 cups shredded Swiss cheese (8 oz)
1 to 2 tablespoons butter or margarine	½ lb thinly sliced corned beef (from deli)
1 cup sliced onions	1 cup sauerkraut, drained, squeezed dry
½ cup salad dressing or mayonnaise	½ to 1 teaspoon caraway seed
4 ½ teaspoons Dijon or Viennese mustard	1 dill pickle, cut crosswise into thin slices

1 Heat oven to 425°F. Lightly grease 12-inch pizza pan or 13×9-inch pan with shortening. Unroll dough; place in pan. Starting at center, press out dough to edge of pan. Bake 9 to 12 minutes or until golden brown.

2 Meanwhile, in 10-inch skillet, melt butter over medium heat. Add onions; cook until tender. In small bowl, mix salad dressing and mustard until well blended.

3 Spread 1/4 cup dressing mixture over partially baked crust. Sprinkle with 1/2 cup of the Swiss cheese. Overlap corned beef slices over cheese and dressing, covering completely. Spread remaining dressing mixture over corned beef. Top evenly with cooked onion slices, sauerkraut and remaining 1 1/2 cups Swiss cheese. Sprinkle with caraway seed.

4 Bake 10 minutes longer or until thoroughly heated and cheese is melted. Garnish with pickle slices.

1 Serving: Calories 370; Total Fat 20g (Saturated Fat 9g; Trans Fat 0g); Cholesterol 65mg; Sodium 1230mg; Total Carbohydrate 30g (Dietary Fiber 1g) • **Exchanges:** 1 Starch, 1 Other Carbohydrate, 2 Medium-Fat Meat, 2 Fat • **Carbohydrate Choices:** 2

Philly Cheese Steak Pizza

Prep Time: **30 Minutes**   Start to Finish: **50 Minutes**   6 servings

1 can (13.8 oz) Pillsbury refrigerated classic pizza crust

1 tablespoon butter or margarine

1 small green bell pepper, cut into thin strips

1 medium onion, halved, thinly sliced

2 cups finely shredded Cheddar cheese (8 oz)

½ lb cooked roast beef (from deli), diced

3 plum (Roma) tomatoes, sliced

1 Heat oven to 425°F. Grease 12-inch pizza pan with shortening. Unroll dough; place in pan. Starting at center, press out dough to edge of pan, forming 1/2-inch rim. Bake 8 to 10 minutes or until light golden brown.

2 Meanwhile, in 8-inch skillet, melt butter over medium-high heat. Add bell pepper and onion; cook 3 to 5 minutes, stirring occasionally, until tender.

3 Sprinkle 1 cup of the cheese evenly over partially baked crust. Top with bell pepper mixture, beef, remaining 1 cup cheese and the tomato slices (be sure beef is completely covered with cheese).

4 Bake 12 to 18 minutes longer or until crust is deep golden brown. Cut into wedges to serve.

1 Serving: Calories 420; Total Fat 18g (Saturated Fat 10g; Trans Fat 0g); Cholesterol 80mg; Sodium 740mg; Total Carbohydrate 35g (Dietary Fiber 0g) • **Exchanges:** 1 ½ Starch, 1 Other Carbohydrate, 3 ½ Lean Meat, 1 Fat • **Carbohydrate Choices:** 2

pizza bites If you do not have a 12-inch pizza pan, just lay the dough out on a cookie sheet. Press the edges up to form a 1/2-inch rim. Continue as directed.

Chicken Fajita Pizza

Bake-Off® Contest 34, 1990   Elizabeth Daniels   Kula, Maui, HI

Prep Time: **20 Minutes**   Start to Finish: **40 Minutes**   8 servings

1 can (13.8 oz) Pillsbury refrigerated classic pizza crust

1 tablespoon olive or vegetable oil

4 boneless skinless chicken breasts (about 1 ¼ lb), cut into thin bite-size strips

1 to 2 teaspoons chili powder

½ to 1 teaspoon salt

½ teaspoon garlic powder

1 cup thinly sliced onions

1 cup green or red bell pepper strips (2×¼ inch)

½ cup chunky-style salsa

2 cups shredded Monterey Jack cheese (8 oz)

1 Heat oven to 425°F. Spray 12-inch pizza pan or 13×9-inch pan with cooking spray. Unroll dough; place in pan. Starting at center, press out dough to edge of pan. Bake 7 to 9 minutes or until very light golden brown.

2 Meanwhile, in 10-inch skillet, heat oil over medium-high heat. Add chicken; sprinkle with chili powder, salt and garlic powder. Cook and stir 3 to 5 minutes or until lightly browned. Add onions and bell pepper strips; cook and stir 2 to 3 minutes longer or until chicken is no longer pink in center and vegetables are crisp-tender. Spoon chicken mixture evenly over partially baked crust. Spoon salsa over chicken; sprinkle with cheese.

3 Bake 14 to 18 minutes longer or until crust is golden brown. Cut into wedges or squares to serve.

1 Serving: Calories 340; Total Fat 14g (Saturated Fat 7g; Trans Fat 0g); Cholesterol 65mg; Sodium 790mg; Total Carbohydrate 27g (Dietary Fiber 0g) • **Exchanges:** 1 ½ Starch, ½ Other Carbohydrate, 3 Lean Meat, ½ Fat • **Carbohydrate Choices:** 2

Chicken Pizza Primavera

Bake-Off® Contest 41, 2004   Janet Burns   Virginia Beach, VA

Prep Time: **15 Minutes**   Start to Finish: **30 Minutes**   4 servings

1 can (13.8 oz) Pillsbury refrigerated classic pizza crust

Olive oil cooking spray

2 tablespoons shredded Asiago cheese

¼ to ½ teaspoon garlic salt

2 tablespoons light ranch dressing

1 package (6 oz) refrigerated cooked Italian-style chicken breast strips, chopped

⅓ cup finely chopped red bell pepper

⅓ cup thinly sliced red onion

½ cup torn baby spinach

1 ½ cups shredded Italian cheese blend (6 oz)

1 teaspoon dried pizza seasoning

1 Heat oven to 400°F. Lightly grease 12-inch pizza pan or pizza stone with shortening or spray with cooking spray. Unroll dough; place in pan or on pizza stone. Starting at center, press out dough to edge of pan or into 12-inch round.

2 Lightly spray dough with olive oil cooking spray. Sprinkle Asiago cheese and garlic salt over dough. Bake 8 to 10 minutes or until lightly browned.

3 Spread ranch dressing over partially baked crust. Top with chicken, bell pepper, onion and spinach. Sprinkle Italian cheese blend and pizza seasoning over top.

4 Bake 9 to 12 minutes longer or until crust is golden brown and cheese is melted. Cut into wedges.

1 Serving: Calories 480; Total Fat 18g (Saturated Fat 9g; Trans Fat 0g); Cholesterol 70mg; Sodium 1570mg; Total Carbohydrate 51g (Dietary Fiber 0g) • **Exchanges:** 2 ½ Starch, 1 Other Carbohydrate, 3 Lean Meat, 1 ½ Fat • **Carbohydrate Choices:** 3 ½

Smoky Chicken Pizza

Prep Time: **20 Minutes**   Start to Finish: **30 Minutes**   4 servings

1 can (13.8 oz) Pillsbury
refrigerated classic pizza crust

2 packages (4 oz each)
refrigerated mesquite
barbecue-flavored boneless
skinless chicken breast fillet

1 can (8 oz) tomato sauce

2 tablespoons hickory smoke-
flavored barbecue sauce

½ cup chopped ripe olives

¼ cup chopped red onion

4 oz provolone cheese,
shredded (1 cup)

¼ cup grated Parmesan cheese

1   Heat oven to 425°F. Grease cookie sheet with shortening. Unroll
dough; place on cookie sheet. Starting at center, press out dough to
form 15×10-inch rectangle. Bake about 7 minutes or until crust just
begins to brown.

2   Meanwhile, cook chicken breast fillets as directed on package. Finely
chop chicken. In small bowl, combine tomato sauce and barbecue
sauce; mix well.

3   Spread tomato sauce mixture over partially baked pizza crust. Top
with chicken, olives, onion and cheeses.

4   Bake 6 to 10 minutes or until crust is deep golden brown and cheese
is melted.

1 Serving: Calories 520; Total Fat 19g (Saturated Fat 8g; Trans Fat 0g); Cholesterol 55mg;
Sodium 1950mg; Total Carbohydrate 58g (Dietary Fiber 1g) • **Exchanges:** 3 Starch,
1 Other Carbohydrate, 3 Medium-Fat Meat • **Carbohydrate Choices:** 4

Grilled Chicken and Cilantro Pizza

Prep Time: **20 Minutes**   Start to Finish: **45 Minutes**   6 servings

2 boneless skinless chicken breasts

¾ cup red chile sauce or chili sauce

1 can (16.3 oz) Pillsbury Grands! Flaky Layers refrigerated original biscuits

¼ to ½ cup fajita sauce

1 tomato, sliced

1 can (4.5 oz) chopped green chiles or ¼ cup chopped fresh Anaheim peppers

1 ½ cups shredded mozzarella cheese (6 oz)

¼ cup chopped fresh cilantro

1   Heat gas or charcoal grill. Remove 1/4 cup of the chili sauce; set remainder aside. Brush chicken with the 1/4 cup of the chili sauce; marinate at room temperature 5 minutes. Place chicken on gas grill over hot heat or on charcoal grill 4 to 6 inches from hot coals. Cook 6 to 8 minutes or until chicken is fork-tender and juices run clear, turning once.

2   Cool chicken; pull into shreds and place in medium bowl. Add remaining chili sauce; mix well.

3   Heat oven to 350°F. Lightly spray large cookie sheet with cooking spray or grease with shortening. Separate dough into 8 biscuits. Arrange biscuit dough on sprayed cookie sheet in a large circle with biscuits overlapping and going toward the center. Press dough to form 1/4-inch thick crust.

4   Spread fajita sauce over crust. Top with shredded chicken, tomato slices, green chiles, and mozzarella cheese and cilantro.

5   Bake 18 to 22 minutes or until cheese in center is melted.

1 Serving: Calories 430; Total Fat 19g (Saturated Fat 7g; Trans Fat 5g); Cholesterol 40mg; Sodium 1740mg; Total Carbohydrate 41g (Dietary Fiber 3g) • **Exchanges:** 2 Starch, 1 Other Carbohydrate, 2 ½ Very Lean Meat, 3 Fat • **Carbohydrate Choices:** 3

Chicken and Spinach Dip Pizza

Prep Time: **15 Minutes**   Start to Finish: **30 Minutes**   8 servings

Cornmeal

1 can (13.8 oz) Pillsbury refrigerated classic pizza crust

1 container (8 oz) refrigerated spinach dip

1 cup chopped cooked chicken

1 large tomato, seeded, chopped (1 cup)

1 cup sliced fresh mushrooms (3 oz)

1 ½ cups shredded mozzarella cheese (6 oz)

1 Heat oven to 400°F. Sprinkle cornmeal on 12-inch pizza stone or pizza pan. Unroll dough; place on pizza stone or pan. Starting at center, press out dough into 12-inch round or to edge of pan, forming 1/2-inch rim. Bake 8 minutes.

2 Spread spinach dip over partially baked crust. Top with chicken, tomato and mushrooms. Sprinkle with cheese.

3 Bake 12 to 15 minutes longer or until crust is golden brown and cheese is melted.

1 Serving: Calories 280; Total Fat 12g (Saturated Fat 6g; Trans Fat 0g); Cholesterol 35mg; Sodium 680mg; Total Carbohydrate 27g (Dietary Fiber 0g) • **Exchanges:** 1 Starch, 1 Other Carbohydrate, 2 Lean Meat, 1 Fat • **Carbohydrate Choices:** 2

Personalized Individual Pizzas

Prep Time: **20 Minutes**   Start to Finish: **35 Minutes**   4 servings

Cornmeal, if desired

1 can (13.8 oz) Pillsbury refrigerated classic pizza crust

2 teaspoons olive oil

¼ cup pizza sauce

¼ cup shredded Cheddar cheese (2 oz)

1 ¼ cups shredded mozzarella cheese (6 oz)

Italian Sausage Pizza

⅛ lb bulk Italian Sausage

½ small onion, chopped (¼ cup)

½ teaspoon chopped fresh oregano, if desired

Margherita Pizza

1 tablespoon shredded Parmesan cheese

3 to 4 (¼-inch-thick) slices plum (Roma) tomato (about 1 medium tomato)

1 tablespoon thin fresh basil strips

Pepperoni Pizza

8 to 10 slices pepperoni (from 3-oz package)

1 Heat oven to 425°F. Spray cookie sheet with cooking spray; sprinkle with cornmeal. Do not unroll dough. Cut roll of dough into 4 equal pieces; shape each piece into a ball. Roll or press each ball of dough into a 5-inch round, making edges slightly thicker to form a rim. Place the rounds on the prepared cookie sheet; brush each with oil.

2 Bake 6 to 8 minutes. Top each round with 1 of the toppings below. Bake 10 to 13 minutes longer or until crust is deep golden brown and cheese is melted and bubbly.

Italian Sausage Pizza: Cook sausage and onion in 8-inch skillet over medium heat, stirring frequently, just until sausage is no longer pink; drain. Spread round with 2 tablespoons pizza sauce. Sprinkle with 1/4 cup mozzarella cheese. Top with sausage and 1/4 cup mozzarella cheese. After baking, sprinkle with oregano.

Margherita Pizza: Sprinkle round with Parmesan cheese and 1/4 cup shredded mozzarella cheese. Top with tomato slices and 1/4 cup shredded mozzarella cheese. After baking, sprinkle with basil strips.

Pepperoni Pizza: Spread round with 2 tablespoons pizza sauce. Mix 1/4 cup Cheddar cheese and 1/4 cup mozzarella cheese; sprinkle over pizza sauce. Top with pepperoni.

1 Serving: Calories 600; Total Fat 27g (Saturated Fat 13g; Trans Fat 0g); Cholesterol 65mg; Sodium 1660mg; Total Carbohydrate 58g (Dietary Fiber 1g) • **Exchanges:** 3 Starch, 1 Other Carbohydrate, 3 Lean Meat, 3 Fat • **Carbohydrate Choices:** 4

Shrimp and Feta Greek-Style Pizza

Bake-Off® Contest 34, 1990   Debbie Vanni   Libertyville, IL

Prep Time: **15 Minutes**   Start to Finish: **35 Minutes**   6 servings

1 lb uncooked medium shrimp in shells

1 tablespoon cornmeal

1 can (13.8 oz) Pillsbury refrigerated classic pizza crust

1 cup shredded mozzarella cheese (4 oz)

1 tablespoon olive oil or vegetable oil

2 cloves garlic, finely chopped

1/2 cup crumbled feta cheese (4 oz)

1/4 cup sliced green onions (4 medium)

1 to 2 teaspoons rosemary, crushed or 1 tablespoon chopped fresh rosemary

1 can (2 1/4 oz) sliced ripe olives, drained

1 Shell and devein shrimp; set aside.

2 Heat oven to 425°F. Grease 12-inch pizza pan or 13×9-inch pan with shortening; sprinkle with cornmeal. Unroll dough; place in pan. Starting at center, press out dough to edge of pan. Sprinkle with mozzarella cheese.

3 In 10-inch skillet, heat olive oil over medium-high heat. Add shrimp and garlic. Cook until shrimp are light pink, about 1 minute, stirring frequently. Spoon over mozzarella cheese. Sprinkle feta cheese, onions, rosemary and olives evenly over shrimp.

4 Bake 18 to 22 minutes or until crust is golden brown.

1 Serving: Calories 330; Total Fat 12g (Saturated Fat 5g; Trans Fat 0g); Cholesterol 90mg; Sodium 870mg; Total Carbohydrate 35g (Dietary Fiber 0g) • **Exchanges:** 1 1/2 Starch, 1 Other Carbohydrate, 2 Medium-Fat Meat • **Carbohydrate Choices:** 2

pizza bites A 12-ounce package frozen medium-sized shrimp, thawed and drained, can be substituted for fresh shrimp.

Cheesy Bean and Chicken Pizza

Bake-Off® Contest 42, 2006   Patrice Kavanagh   Easton, PA

Prep Time: **15 Minutes**   Start to Finish: **30 Minutes**   6 servings

1 can (13.8 oz) Pillsbury refrigerated classic pizza crust

¾ cup regular or reduced-fat mayonnaise

1 teaspoon lime or lemon juice

1 can (4.5 oz) chopped green chiles, drained

1 can (15 or 15.5 oz) kidney beans, well drained

1 cup shredded cooked chicken

1 ½ cups shredded Mexican cheese blend (6 oz)

2 tablespoons chopped fresh cilantro, if desired

1 Heat oven to 425°F. Lightly grease 14-inch pizza pan with shortening or cooking spray. Unroll dough; place in pan. Starting at center, press out dough to edge of pan. Bake 8 to 10 minutes or until crust just begins to brown around edge.

2 Meanwhile, in small bowl, mix mayonnaise, lime juice and chiles.

3 Gently spread mayonnaise mixture over partially baked crust. Top with beans, chicken and cheese. Bake 10 to 14 minutes longer or until crust is golden brown. Sprinkle with cilantro before serving.

1 Serving: Calories 590; Total Fat 34g (Saturated Fat 10g; Trans Fat 0g); Cholesterol 60mg; Sodium 1290mg; Total Carbohydrate 47g (Dietary Fiber 4g) • **Exchanges:** 2 Starch, 1 Other Carbohydrate, 2 ½ Medium-Fat Meat, 4 Fat • **Carbohydrate Choices:** 3

pizza bites If you have cooked beef or pork on hand, use 1 cup shredded or chopped for the 1 cup shredded chicken.

Margherita Pizza

Prep Time: **25 Minutes**   Start to Finish: **45 Minutes**   8 servings

2 teaspoons cornmeal

1 can (13.8 oz) Pillsbury refrigerated classic pizza crust

2 teaspoons olive oil

1 teaspoon minced garlic

1 ½ cups shredded mozzarella cheese (6 oz)

¼ cup shredded Parmesan cheese

6 medium plum (Roma) tomatoes, cut into 1/4-inch slices

⅓ cup thin fresh basil strips

1 Place oven rack in lowest rack position; heat oven to 425°F. Spray 15×10-inch pan with cooking spray; sprinkle with cornmeal. Unroll dough; place in pan. Starting at center, press out dough to edge of pan. Brush dough with oil; sprinkle evenly with garlic. Bake 6 to 8 minutes or until set and dry.

2 Sprinkle mozzarella and Parmesan cheeses over partially baked crust. Arrange tomato slices over cheese. Sprinkle with half of the basil.

3 Return pizza to lowest oven rack; bake 12 to 17 minutes longer or until crust is deep golden brown. Sprinkle remaining half of basil over pizza.

1 Serving: Calories 220; Total Fat 8g (Saturated Fat 4g; Trans Fat 0g); Cholesterol 15mg; Sodium 520mg; Total Carbohydrate 27g (Dietary Fiber 0g) • **Exchanges:** 1 ½ Starch, ½ Other Carbohydrate, 1 Fat • **Carbohydrate Choices:** 2

pizza bites Fresh basil, unmistakable for its anise-like aroma, blends beautifully with mozzarella and tomato.

Four-Cheese Pizza

Prep Time: **10 Minutes**   Start to Finish: **30 Minutes**   4 servings

1 can (13.8 oz) Pillsbury refrigerated classic pizza crust

⅓ cup shredded Parmesan cheese

1 tablespoon dried basil leaves

4 oz provolone cheese, shredded (1 cup)

1 cup shredded Cheddar cheese (4 oz)

1 cup shredded Monterey Jack cheese (4 oz)

½ cup pasta sauce

1 Heat oven to 425°F. Grease 12-inch pizza pan or 13×9-inch pan with shortening. Unroll dough; place in pan. Starting at center, press out dough to edge of pan, forming 1/2-inch rim. Bake 7 to 9 minutes or until light golden brown.

2 Sprinkle Parmesan cheese and basil over partially baked crust. Top with provolone, Cheddar and Monterey Jack cheese. Spoon spaghetti sauce over cheese.

3 Bake 12 to 18 minutes or until crust is deep golden brown.

1 Serving: Calories 640; Total Fat 32g (Saturated Fat 19g; Trans Fat 0.5g); Cholesterol 80mg; Sodium 1580mg; Total Carbohydrate 54g (Dietary Fiber 0g) • **Exchanges:** 2 ½ Starch, 1 Other Carbohydrate, 3 ½ High-Fat Meat, ½ Fat • **Carbohydrate Choices:** 3 ½

pizza bites If you have fresh basil, use 1/4 cup chopped for the 1 tablespoon dried basil.

Three-Pepper Pizza

Prep Time: **10 Minutes**   Start to Finish: **25 Minutes**   3 servings

1 can (13.8 oz) Pillsbury refrigerated classic pizza crust	1 medium green bell pepper, chopped
1 ½ cups shredded mozzarella cheese (6 oz)	1 medium red bell pepper, chopped
½ teaspoon Italian seasoning	1 medium yellow bell pepper, chopped

1 Heat oven to 425°F. Lightly grease 12-inch pizza pan or 13×9-inch pan with shortening. Unroll dough; place in pan. Starting at center, press out dough to edge of pan. Bake 4 to 6 minutes or until crust just begins to brown.

2 Sprinkle 1/2 cup of the cheese evenly over partially baked crust. Sprinkle with Italian seasoning. Sprinkle peppers evenly over top. Sprinkle with remaining 1 cup cheese.

3 Bake 8 to 12 minutes longer or until crust is deep golden brown and cheese is melted.

1 Serving: Calories 530; Total Fat 16g (Saturated Fat 8g; Trans Fat 0g); Cholesterol 30mg; Sodium 1240mg; Total Carbohydrate 71g (Dietary Fiber 2g) • **Exchanges:** 3 ½ Starch, 1 Other Carbohydrate, 1 Vegetable, 2 Medium-Fat Meat, ½ Fat • **Carbohydrate Choices:** 5

Grilled Fresh Vegetable Pizza

Prep Time: **30 Minutes**   Start to Finish: **30 Minutes**   4 servings

1 cup fresh small broccoli florets

1 can (13.8 oz) Pillsbury refrigerated classic pizza crust

2 teaspoons olive or vegetable oil

1 small yellow summer squash, sliced lengthwise

½ cup pizza sauce

2 plum (Roma) tomatoes, sliced

1 ½ cups shredded mozzarella cheese (6 oz)

1   Heat gas or charcoal grill. In small microwavable bowl, combine broccoli and 3 tablespoons water; cover with microwavable plastic wrap. Microwave on High 2 to 3 minutes or until broccoli is bright green. Drain; set aside.

2   Cut 18×12-inch sheet of heavy-duty foil; spray with cooking spray. Unroll dough; place on foil. Starting at center, press out dough to form 13×9-inch rectangle. Brush dough with 1 teaspoon of the oil. Brush squash with remaining teaspoon oil.

3   When ready to grill, place squash on grill. Invert dough onto grill rack and peel off foil. Cook on gas grill over medium-low heat or on charcoal grill over medium-low coals for 3 to 5 minutes or until bottom of dough is golden brown and squash is crisp-tender and grill-marked, turning squash occasionally.

4   Remove squash from grill; place on cutting board. Cut squash into bite-sized pieces. Turn dough; grill 1 to 2 minutes or until bottom is set. Carefully remove from grill. Top crust with pizza sauce, tomatoes, squash and broccoli. Sprinkle with cheese.

5   Return pizza to grill. Cook 3 to 5 minutes longer or until crust is browned and thoroughly cooked, and cheese is melted.

1 Serving: Calories 420; Total Fat 14g (Saturated Fat 6g; Trans Fat 0g); Cholesterol 25mg; Sodium 1070mg; Total Carbohydrate 54g (Dietary Fiber 1g) • **Exchanges:** 3 Starch, ½ Other Carbohydrate, 1 ½ Medium-Fat Meat, 1 Fat • **Carbohydrate Choices:** 3 ½

Spinach Pierogi Pizza

Bake-Off® Contest 36, 1994   Rebecca Jo Verdone   Greensburg, PA

Prep Time: **20 Minutes**   Start to Finish: **40 Minutes**   8 servings

1 can (13.8 oz) Pillsbury refrigerated classic pizza crust

1 box (9 oz) frozen spinach in a pouch, thawed, squeezed to drain

½ cup chopped onion

2 tablespoons butter or margarine

1 ½ cups mashed potatoes

2 tablespoons oil

½ teaspoon garlic salt

1 cup shredded mozzarella cheese (4 oz)

½ cup shredded Cheddar cheese (2 oz)

1 small onion, sliced, separated into rings

1 Heat oven to 425°F. Grease 13×9-inch pan with shortening. Unroll dough; place in pan. Starting at center, press out dough to edge of pan. Bake 8 to 10 minutes or until light golden brown.

2 Meanwhile, in 10-inch skillet, cook spinach and chopped onion in butter until onion is crisp-tender. Stir in potatoes; mix well. In small bowl, combine oil and garlic salt; mix well. Brush over partially baked crust; top with spinach mixture. Sprinkle with mozzarella cheese and then Cheddar cheese. Top with onion rings.

3 Bake 15 to 20 minutes or until edges of crust are golden brown and cheese is melted.

1 Serving: Calories 320; Total Fat 15g (Saturated Fat 6g; Trans Fat 0.5g); Cholesterol 25mg; Sodium 650mg; Total Carbohydrate 34g (Dietary Fiber 2g) • **Exchanges:** 1 ½ Starch, 1 Other Carbohydrate, 1 High-Fat Meat, 1 Fat • **Carbohydrate Choices:** 2

pizza bites The stuffed noodle dumplings called pierogi are a Polish specialty. This pizza uses two popular Pierogi fillings: spinach and mashed potatoes.

2 Pizza for Get-Togethers

Rise 'n Shine Lattice Pizza

Bake-Off® Contest 42 , 2006   Maria Baldwin   Mesa, AZ

Prep Time: **35 Minutes**   Start to Finish: **1 Hour 15 Minutes**   8 servings

1 box (9 oz) frozen roasted potatoes with garlic & herbs

½ cup chives-and-onion cream cheese spread (from 8-oz container)

1 teaspoon Italian seasoning

2 eggs

¾ to 1 cup basil pesto

1 can (13.8 oz) Pillsbury refrigerated classic pizza crust

2 cups grated Asiago or Parmesan cheese (8 oz)

1 package or jar (3 oz) cooked real bacon bits or pieces

1 box (10.6 oz) Pillsbury refrigerated Italian garlic with herbs breadsticks

1 Heat oven to 350°F. Cut small slit in center of pouch of potatoes. Microwave on High 2 to 3 minutes or just until warm; set aside. In small bowl, beat cream cheese, Italian seasoning and eggs with electric mixer on medium speed until well blended; set aside.

2 Line large cookie sheet with cooking parchment paper. Place pesto in small strainer over bowl to drain. Lightly brush oil from pesto onto parchment paper. Unroll pizza crust dough; place on paper-lined cookie sheet. Starting at center, press out dough into 14-inch square.

3 Spread pesto over dough to within 1 inch of edges; sprinkle with cheese. Roll up edges of dough to make 11-inch square. Spoon potatoes over cheese; pour eggs over potatoes. Sprinkle with bacon.

4 Separate breadstick dough into 10 strips; set garlic butter aside. Twist and stretch each strip of dough over potatoes in lattice pattern, tucking ends under pizza dough. Remove cover from garlic butter; microwave on High 10 seconds to soften. Brush garlic butter over dough.

5 Bake 30 minutes or until edges are browned and center is set, covering with foil last 10 minutes. Immediately remove from cookie sheet.

1 Serving: Calories 600; Total Fat 36g (Saturated Fat 13g; Trans Fat 1.5g); Cholesterol 120mg; Sodium 1670mg; Total Carbohydrate 47g (Dietary Fiber 2g) • **Exchanges:** 2 Starch, 1 Other Carbohydrate, 2 ½ Medium-Fat Meat, 4 ½ Fat • **Carbohydrate Choices:** 3

Ham and Chile Brunch Pizza

Bake-Off® Contest 40, 2002   Jennifer Kavanagh   Easton, PA

Prep Time: **15 Minutes**   Start to Finish: **30 Minutes**   4 servings

1 can (13.8 oz) Pillsbury refrigerated classic pizza crust

6 eggs

¼ teaspoon salt

⅛ teaspoon pepper

1 tablespoon butter

1 cup julienne-cut strips or chopped cooked ham

1 can (4.5 oz) chopped green chiles

1 ½ cups shredded Monterey Jack cheese (6 oz)

2 tablespoons chopped fresh cilantro, if desired

1 Heat oven to 425°F. Grease 14-inch pizza pan with shortening. Unroll dough; place in pan. Starting at center, press out dough to edge of pan. Bake 6 to 8 minutes or until crust begins to brown.

2 Meanwhile, in medium bowl with wire whisk, beat eggs, salt and pepper. In 10-inch skillet, melt butter over medium heat. Add eggs; cook 1 to 2 minutes, stirring frequently, until firm but still moist.

3 Spoon and spread eggs over partially baked crust. Top with ham, chiles and cheese.

4 Bake 8 to 12 minutes longer or until crust is deep golden brown. Sprinkle with cilantro before serving.

1 Serving: Calories 610; Total Fat 30g (Saturated Fat 14g; Trans Fat 0g); Cholesterol 385mg; Sodium 2170mg; Total Carbohydrate 49g (Dietary Fiber 0g) • **Exchanges:** 2 Starch, 1 Other Carbohydrate, 4 Medium-Fat Meat, 2 Fat • **Carbohydrate Choices:** 3

pizza bites Add a little kick and use 1 1/2 cups shredded hot pepper Monterey Jack cheese.

Canadian Bacon–Apple Pizza

Bake-Off® Contest 41, 2004   Arlene Swiatek Gillen   Holland, NY

Prep Time: **15 Minutes**   Start to Finish: **35 Minutes**   16 servings

4 teaspoons sesame seed

1 can (13.8 oz) Pillsbury refrigerated classic pizza crust

2 ½ tablespoons horseradish mustard

¼ teaspoon dried thyme leaves

¾ lb thinly sliced Canadian bacon

2 large tart green apples, peeled, sliced (3 cups)

1 package (8 oz) deli-thin Swiss cheese slices

1 Heat oven to 400°F. Grease large cookie sheet with shortening or spray with cooking spray. Sprinkle sesame seed onto cookie sheet. Unroll dough; place on cookie sheet over seed. Starting at center, press out dough into 16×13-inch rectangle.

2 Spread mustard over dough; sprinkle evenly with thyme. Layer bacon, apples and cheese over mustard, covering entire surface.

3 Bake 14 to 18 minutes or until crust is golden brown and cheese is melted. Cut into 16 squares.

1 Serving: Calories 170; Total Fat 7g (Saturated Fat 3.5g; Trans Fat 0g); Cholesterol 25mg; Sodium 560mg; Total Carbohydrate 16g (Dietary Fiber 0g) • **Exchanges:** 1 Starch, 1 High-Fat Meat • **Carbohydrate Choices:** 1

pizza bites For a crispier crust, bake crust 11 to 16 minutes or until lightly browned, then add toppings; bake pizza 4 to 7 minutes longer.

Canadian Bacon and Pineapple Pizza

Prep Time: **15 Minutes**   Start to Finish: **35 Minutes**   8 servings

1 can (13.8 oz) Pillsbury refrigerated classic pizza crust

1 package (6 oz) sliced provolone cheese

1 package (5 to 6 oz) sliced Canadian bacon

1 can (8 oz) pineapple chunks in unsweetened juice, well drained on paper towels

$\frac{1}{2}$ cup thinly sliced red onion

$\frac{1}{2}$ cup chopped green bell pepper

$\frac{1}{2}$ cup shredded Cheddar cheese (2 oz)

1 Heat oven to 425°F. Spray 12-inch pizza pan or 13×9-inch pan with cooking spray. Unroll dough; place in pan. Starting at center, press out dough to edge of pan.

2 Top dough with provolone cheese, cutting to fit. Arrange Canadian bacon, pineapple, onion and bell pepper over cheese to within 1/2 inch of edges. Sprinkle with Cheddar cheese.

3 Bake 16 to 20 minutes longer or until crust is deep golden brown.

1 Serving: Calories 280; Total Fat 11g (Saturated Fat 6g; Trans Fat 0g); Cholesterol 30mg; Sodium 860mg; Total Carbohydrate 29g (Dietary Fiber 0g) • **Exchanges:** 1 ½ Starch, ½ Other Carbohydrate, 1 ½ Medium-Fat Meat, ½ Fat • **Carbohydrate Choices:** 2

pizza bites For a crispier crust, bake crust 6 to 8 minutes or until crust is set and dry, then add toppings; bake pizza 12 to 16 minutes longer.

Deluxe Turkey Club Pizza

Bake-Off® Contest 35, 1992   Teresa Hannan Smith   Sacramento, CA

Prep Time: **25 Minutes**   Start to Finish: **35 Minutes**   6 servings

1 can (13.8 oz) Pillsbury refrigerated classic pizza crust

2 teaspoons sesame seed

6 slices bacon, cut into 1-inch pieces

¼ cup light or regular mayonnaise

½ to 1 teaspoon grated lemon peel

1 cup shredded Monterey Jack cheese (4 oz)

1 tablespoon thinly sliced fresh basil or 1 teaspoon dried basil leaves

¼ lb cooked turkey breast slices, cut into 1-inch strips

2 small plum (Roma) tomatoes or 1 small tomato, thinly sliced

½ cup shredded Swiss cheese (2 oz)

Fresh basil leaves, if desired

1 Heat oven to 425°F. Lightly spray 12-inch pizza pan or 13×9-inch pan with cooking spray. Unroll dough; place in pan. Starting at center, press out dough to edge of pan. Sprinkle sesame seed evenly over dough. Bake 10 to 12 minutes or until crust is light golden brown.

2 Meanwhile, in 10-inch skillet, cook bacon over medium heat until crisp. Remove bacon from skillet; drain on paper towels. In small bowl, mix mayonnaise and lemon peel until well blended.

3 Spread mayonnaise mixture over partially baked crust. Top with Monterey Jack cheese, sliced basil, turkey, cooked bacon and tomatoes; sprinkle with Swiss cheese.

4 Bake 7 to 9 minutes longer or until crust is golden brown and cheese is melted. Garnish with fresh basil leaves.

1 Serving: Calories 380; Total Fat 18g (Saturated Fat 8g; Trans Fat 0g); Cholesterol 55mg; Sodium 850mg; Total Carbohydrate 34g (Dietary Fiber 0g) • **Exchanges:** 1 ½ Starch, ½ Other Carbohydrate, 2 ½ Medium-Fat Meat, 1 Fat • **Carbohydrate Choices:** 2

Mandarin Chicken Salad Pizza

Bake-Off® Contest 39, 2000   Elizabeth Hauerwas   Manhattan, KS

Prep Time: **30 Minutes**   Start to Finish: **30 Minutes**   8 servings

1 can (13.8 oz) Pillsbury refrigerated classic pizza crust

1 can (9.7 oz) chunk white chicken breast in water, drained

¾ cup Oriental salad dressing

¼ cup mayonnaise or salad dressing

3 medium green onions, chopped (3 tablespoons)

1 cup shredded Monterey Jack cheese (4 oz)

3 cups shredded romaine lettuce

½ cup chow mein noodles

1 can (11 oz) mandarin orange segments, drained

1 Heat oven to 425°F. Grease cookie sheet with shortening. Unroll dough; place on cookie sheet. Starting at center, press out dough into 12x8-inch rectangle. Bake 7 to 9 minutes or until light golden brown.

2 Meanwhile, in medium bowl, combine chicken, 1/4 cup of the salad dressing, mayonnaise and onions; mix well.

3 Spread chicken mixture evenly over partially baked crust. Sprinkle with cheese. Bake 6 to 8 minutes longer or until crust is deep golden brown and cheese is melted.

4 Meanwhile, in large bowl, combine lettuce, chow mein noodles, mandarin orange segments and remaining 1/2 cup salad dressing; mix well. Top each serving with salad mixture.

1 Serving: Calories 280; Total Fat 12g (Saturated Fat 4g; Trans Fat 0g); Cholesterol 30mg; Sodium 810mg; Total Carbohydrate 30g (Dietary Fiber 1g) • **Exchanges:** 1 ½ Starch, ½ Other Carbohydrate, 1 Lean Meat, 1 ½ Fat • **Carbohydrate Choices:** 2

Orange-Chicken-Chipotle Pizza

Bake-Off® Contest 41, 2004   April Carty-Sipp   Collingswood, NJ

Prep Time: **15 Minutes**   Start to Finish: **30 Minutes**   6 servings

1 can (13.8 oz) Pillsbury refrigerated classic pizza crust

2 tablespoons extra-virgin olive oil

1 large onion, quartered, sliced

3 boneless skinless chicken breasts, cut into ½-inch pieces

⅓ cup orange marmalade

1 teaspoon seasoned salt

1 teaspoon ground cumin

1 to 3 chipotle chiles in adobo sauce (from 7-oz can), finely chopped

1 can (11 oz) mandarin orange segments, well drained on paper towels

1 cup shredded Monterey Jack cheese (4 oz)

1 cup shredded sharp Cheddar cheese (4 oz)

1 Heat oven to 425°F. Lightly spray 14-inch pizza pan with cooking spray. Unroll dough; place in pan. Starting at center, press out dough to edge of pan. Bake 6 to 8 minutes or until crust just begins to brown.

2 Meanwhile, in 10-inch skillet, heat oil over medium heat until hot. Cook onion in oil 6 to 8 minutes, stirring frequently, until caramelized.

3 Reduce oven temperature to 375°F. Add chicken to skillet; cook 5 to 6 minutes, stirring frequently, until chicken is no longer pink in center. Stir in marmalade, salt, cumin, chipotle chiles and mandarin orange segments. Remove from heat; cool 1 minute.

4 Spread chicken mixture evenly over partially baked crust. Sprinkle both cheeses over top. Bake at 375°F 10 to 13 minutes or until cheese is melted and crust is deep golden brown.

1 Serving: Calories 500; Total Fat 21g (Saturated Fat 9g; Trans Fat 0g); Cholesterol 75mg; Sodium 1010mg; Total Carbohydrate 51g (Dietary Fiber 1g) • **Exchanges:** 2 Starch, 1 ½ Other Carbohydrate, 3 Very Lean Meat, 3 ½ Fat • **Carbohydrate Choices:** 3 ½

Chicken and Artichoke Pizza

Prep Time: **15 Minutes**   Start to Finish: **35 Minutes**   8 servings

1 can (13.8 oz) Pillsbury refrigerated classic pizza crust

¼ cup creamy Caesar salad dressing

3 tablespoons grated Parmesan cheese

2 cups chopped cooked chicken

1 jar (6 to 7 oz) marinated artichoke hearts, drained, coarsely chopped

6 oz fontina cheese, shredded (1 ½ cups)

2 plum (Roma) tomatoes, seeded, chopped

1 Heat oven to 400°F. Lightly grease 12-inch pizza pan with shortening. Unroll dough; place in pan. Starting at center, press out dough to edge of pan. Bake 6 to 8 minutes or until crust begins to dry.

2 Meanwhile, in small bowl, combine salad dressing and Parmesan cheese.

3 Spread dressing mixture over partially baked crust. Top with chicken and artichokes. Sprinkle with fontina cheese. Top with tomatoes.

4 Bake 15 to 20 minutes longer or until crust is golden brown and cheese is melted. Cut into wedges to serve.

1 Serving: Calories 330; Total Fat 16g (Saturated Fat 6g; Trans Fat 0g); Cholesterol 55mg; Sodium 730mg; Total Carbohydrate 27g (Dietary Fiber 1g) • **Exchanges:** 1 ½ Starch, ½ Other Carbohydrate, 2 ½ Lean Meat, 1 Fat • **Carbohydrate Choices:** 2

pizza bites Don't have a pizza pan? On a lightly greased cookie sheet, press out dough to form 13×9-inch rectangle. Bake at 400°F 5 to 7 minutes. Top partially baked crust with dressing mixture and toppings. Bake 10 to 12 minutes longer.

Mojo Black Bean–Chicken Pizza

Bake-Off® Contest 42, 2006   Ginny Solomon   Brooksville, FL

Prep Time: **20 Minutes**   Start to Finish: **45 Minutes**   8 servings

¼ **cup chopped fresh cilantro or parsley**

¼ **cup mojo criollo marinade (Spanish marinating sauce) or zesty Italian dressing**

½ **small red onion (halved lengthwise), cut into very thin strips**

¼ **teaspoon kosher (coarse) salt**

⅛ **teaspoon cracked black pepper**

1 **can (15 oz) black beans, drained, rinsed**

1 **package (6 oz) refrigerated grilled chicken strips**

1 **can (13.8 oz) Pillsbury refrigerated classic pizza crust**

¾ **cup shredded Monterey Jack cheese (3 oz)**

¾ **cup shredded mozzarella cheese (3 oz)**

1 Heat oven to 400°F. In medium bowl, mix cilantro, marinade, onion, salt, pepper, beans and chicken. Let stand 10 to 15 minutes to marinate.

2 Meanwhile, lightly spray large cookie sheet with cooking spray. Unroll dough; place on cookie sheet. Starting in center, press out dough into 15×11-inch rectangle.

3 Spread chicken mixture over dough to within 1/2 inch of edges. Sprinkle both cheeses over top.

4 Bake 18 to 22 minutes or until crust is golden brown around edges and cheese is melted. Cut into 8 rectangles.

1 Serving: Calories 290; Total Fat 8g (Saturated Fat 4g; Trans Fat 0g); Cholesterol 30mg; Sodium 800mg; Total Carbohydrate 37g (Dietary Fiber 5g) • **Exchanges:** 2 Starch, ½ Other Carbohydrate, 1 ½ Very Lean Meat, 1 Fat • **Carbohydrate Choices:** 2 ½

pizza bites One large boneless skinless chicken breast, grilled and cut into thin strips, can be substituted for the refrigerated grilled chicken strips.

Chicken Waldorf Pizza

Bake-Off® Contest 39, 2000   Ernie Crow   Rockville, MD

Prep Time: **15 Minutes**   Start to Finish: **30 Minutes**   6 servings

1 can (13.8 oz) Pillsbury refrigerated classic pizza crust

1 cup chopped cooked chicken

1 cup chopped apple

½ cup sliced almonds, toasted*

½ cup mayonnaise or salad dressing

1 teaspoon dried tarragon leaves

⅛ teaspoon salt

⅛ teaspoon pepper

2 cups shredded Swiss cheese (8 oz)

2 teaspoons chopped green onions

1 Heat oven to 425°F. Lightly spray 14-inch pizza pan with cooking spray. Unroll dough; place in pan. Starting at center, press out dough to edge of pan. Bake 6 to 8 minutes or until crust just begins to brown.

2 Meanwhile, in medium bowl, mix chicken, apple, almonds, mayonnaise, tarragon, salt and pepper. Spread mixture evenly over partially baked crust. Sprinkle with cheese.

3 Bake 10 to 12 minutes longer or until crust is deep golden brown and cheese is melted. Sprinkle with onions. Cut into 12 wedges.

1 Serving: Calories 540; Total Fat 32g (Saturated Fat 10g; Trans Fat 0g); Cholesterol 60mg; Sodium 720mg; Total Carbohydrate 38g (Dietary Fiber 1g) • **Exchanges:** 2 Starch, ½ Other Carbohydrate, 2 ½ Lean Meat, 4 ½ Fat • **Carbohydrate Choices:** 2 ½

*To toast almonds, spread in a single layer on a cookie sheet and bake at 350°F 5 to 7 minutes or until aromatic and golden, shaking pan occasionally.

pizza bites A large cookie sheet can be used in place of the 14-inch pizza pan. Spray the cookie sheet with cooking spray; press and shape the dough on the sheet into a 14-inch circle or square.

Chicken Cordon Bleu Pizza

Bake-Off® Contest 40, 2002   Merrill Degroo   Belgrade, MT

Prep Time: **15 Minutes**   Start to Finish: **40 Minutes**   4 servings

1 can (13.8 oz) Pillsbury refrigerated classic pizza crust

⅓ cup garlic ranch salad dressing

4 oz smoked provolone cheese, shredded (1 cup)

4 oz refrigerated roasted chicken breast strips

2 oz sliced Canadian bacon, halved

2 tablespoons cooked real bacon pieces

4 medium green onions, sliced (¼ cup)

¼ cup chopped seeded tomato

1 cup shredded mozzarella cheese (4 oz)

1 Heat oven to 425°F. Grease 12-inch pizza pan with shortening. Unroll dough; place in pan. Starting at center, press out dough to edge of pan.

2 Spread salad dressing over crust. Sprinkle with provolone cheese. Top with chicken, Canadian bacon, bacon, onions, tomato and mozzarella cheese.

3 Bake 18 to 22 minutes or until crust is deep golden brown. Cut into wedges to serve.

1 Serving: Calories 610; Total Fat 29g (Saturated Fat 12g; Trans Fat 0g); Cholesterol 70mg; Sodium 1850mg; Total Carbohydrate 52g (Dietary Fiber 0g) • **Exchanges:** 2 ½ Starch, 1 Other Carbohydrate, 3 ½ Medium-Fat Meat, 2 Fat • **Carbohydrate Choices:** 3 ½

Oriental Stir-Fry Pizza

Bake-Off® Contest 35, 1992   Barbara Benton   Ormond Beach, FL

Prep Time: **25 Minutes**   Start to Finish: **40 Minutes**   8 servings

1 can (13.8 oz) Pillsbury refrigerated classic pizza crust

4 boneless skinless chicken breasts, cut into 2×¼-inch strips

½ cup purchased zesty Italian salad dressing

⅓ cup plum jelly or apricot preserves

¼ cup chili sauce

2 tablespoons dry white wine or chicken broth

1 teaspoon lemon juice

½ teaspoon allspice

¼ teaspoon instant minced onion

1 cup sliced fresh mushrooms

1 medium green bell pepper, cut into thin bite-sized strips

1 medium onion, halved, cut into thin bite-sized strips

1 cup shredded hot pepper Monterey Jack cheese (4 oz)

1 cup shredded mozzarella cheese (4 oz)

1 Heat oven to 425°F. Lightly grease 15×10-inch baking pan with shortening. Unroll dough; place in pan. Starting at center, press out dough to edge of pan. Bake 8 to 10 minutes or until light golden brown. Remove partially baked crust from oven. Spread jelly mixture over crust to within 1 inch of edges.

2 Meanwhile, in medium bowl, combine chicken and salad dressing; toss to coat. Set aside. In small saucepan, combine jelly, chili sauce, wine, lemon juice, allspice and instant minced onion; mix well. Bring to a boil. Reduce heat to medium; simmer 5 minutes, stirring frequently.

3 Drain chicken; discard marinade. In large skillet, cook chicken over medium-high heat for 3 minutes, stirring frequently. Add mushrooms, bell pepper and onion; cook and stir 3 to 5 minutes or until vegetables are crisp-tender and chicken is no longer pink in center. Drain well. Spread chicken mixture over jelly mixture. Sprinkle with cheeses.

4 Bake 7 to 12 minutes longer or until crust is golden brown and cheese is melted.

1 Serving: Calories 340; Total Fat 10g (Saturated Fat 5g; Trans Fat 0g); Cholesterol 55mg; Sodium 720mg; Total Carbohydrate 37g (Dietary Fiber 1g) • **Exchanges:** 2 Starch, ½ Other Carbohydrate, 2 ½ Very Lean Meat, 1 ½ Fat • **Carbohydrate Choices:** 2 ½

Chicken Curry Pizza

Bake-Off® Contest 35, 1992   Sharada N. Patil   Rochester, NY

Prep Time: **25 Minutes**   Start to Finish: **55 Minutes**   6 to 8 servings

1 can (13.8 oz) Pillsbury refrigerated classic pizza crust

2 tablespoons vegetable oil

½ lb boneless skinless chicken breast, cut into ¼-inch slices

1 cup chopped onions

½ cup chopped red bell pepper

2 cloves garlic, finely chopped

½ teaspoon salt

¼ teaspoon ground coriander

¼ teaspoon cumin seed

¼ teaspoon grated gingerroot or ground ginger

⅛ teaspoon ground turmeric

⅛ teaspoon ground red pepper (cayenne)

⅛ teaspoon ground cinnamon

⅛ teaspoon ground cloves

1 cup chopped tomato

½ cup frozen sweet peas (from 1-lb bag), thawed

1 cup shredded mozzarella cheese (4 oz)

1 Heat oven to 350°F. Lightly grease 13×9-inch pan or 12-inch pizza pan with shortening. Unroll dough; place in pan. Starting at center, press out dough to edge of pan. Bake 15 to 20 minutes or until light golden brown.

2 Meanwhile, in 10-inch skillet, heat oil over medium-high heat until hot. Add chicken, onions, bell pepper, garlic, salt, coriander, cumin seed, gingerroot, turmeric, red pepper, cinnamon and cloves. Cook and stir 6 to 8 minutes or until chicken is no longer pink and onions are tender. Add tomato and peas; cook and stir about 3 minutes or until tomato is soft. Spread chicken mixture over partially baked crust; sprinkle with cheese.

3 Bake 17 to 22 minutes longer or until edges of crust are golden brown and cheese is melted. Let stand 10 minutes before serving.

1 Serving: Calories 340; Total Fat 12g (Saturated Fat 4g; Trans Fat 0g); Cholesterol 35mg; Sodium 800mg; Total Carbohydrate 38g (Dietary Fiber 1g) • **Exchanges:** 2 Starch, ½ Other Carbohydrate, 2 Very Lean Meat, 2 Fat • **Carbohydrate Choices:** 2 ½

Spicy Mexican Pizza

Bake-Off® Contest 41, 2004   Tamara Strange   Winder, GA

Prep Time: **20 Minutes**   Start to Finish: **40 Minutes**   8 servings

1 can (13.8 oz) Pillsbury refrigerated classic pizza crust

½ lb chorizo sausage (not smoked)

1 can (8 oz) tomato sauce

½ to 1 chipotle chile in adobo sauce (from 7-oz can)

¼ cup chopped fresh cilantro

1 can (2.25 oz) sliced ripe olives, drained

2 cups shredded Colby-Monterey Jack cheese blend (8 oz)

1 Heat oven to 400°F. Grease 15×10-inch pan with shortening or spray with cooking spray. Unroll dough; place in pan. Starting at center, press out dough to edge of pan. Prick dough 15 to 20 times evenly with fork.

2 Meanwhile, remove sausage from casings; place in 10-inch skillet. Cook over medium-high heat, stirring frequently and breaking up sausage, until no longer pink. Remove sausage from skillet; drain well on paper towels. In blender, puree tomato sauce and chipotle chile until smooth.

3 Spread tomato sauce mixture evenly over dough. Sprinkle cooked sausage, cilantro, olives and cheese over sauce.

4 Bake 15 to 18 minutes or until crust is golden brown and cheese is melted. Cut into squares.

1 Serving: Calories 380; Total Fat 22g (Saturated Fat 10g; Trans Fat 0g); Cholesterol 50mg; Sodium 1090mg; Total Carbohydrate 27g (Dietary Fiber 0g) • **Exchanges:** 1 Starch, 1 Other Carbohydrate, 2 High-Fat Meat, 1 Fat • **Carbohydrate Choices:** 2

pizza bites For a crispier crust, bake crust 8 to 10 minutes or until very light brown, then add toppings; bake pizza 12 to 15 minutes longer.

Maui Paradise Pizza

Bake-Off® Contest 38, 1998   Sharon Ogawa   Riverside, CA

Prep Time: **30 Minutes**   Start to Finish: **30 Minutes**   8 servings

Crust

1 can (13.8 oz) Pillsbury refrigerated classic pizza crust

¼ cup chopped macadamia nuts

Topping

½ lb cooked deveined peeled small shrimp, thawed if frozen, tail shells removed

1 tablespoon fresh lime juice

1 teaspoon finely chopped serrano or jalapeño chile

¼ teaspoon salt

¼ teaspoon white pepper

½ cup chopped peeled mango

½ cup chopped peeled kiwifruit (1 kiwifruit)

½ cup chopped red bell pepper

½ cup pineapple tidbits, well drained (from 8-oz can)

¼ to ½ cup thinly sliced green onions (4 to 8 medium)

¼ to ½ cup chopped red onion

⅓ cup chopped fresh cilantro

1 package (8 oz) cream cheese, softened

6 red bell pepper rings, if desired

Fresh cilantro sprigs, if desired

1 Heat oven to 425°F. Grease 12-inch pizza pan or 13×9-inch pan with shortening. Unroll dough; place in pan. Starting at center, press out dough to edge of pan. Press nuts around edge. Bake 8 to 12 minutes or until golden brown. Cool 10 to 15 minutes.

2 Meanwhile, in large bowl, combine shrimp, lime juice, chile, salt and pepper; mix well. Let stand to marinate while chopping fruits and vegetables. Add mango, kiwifruit, chopped bell pepper, pineapple, green onions, red onion and chopped cilantro; mix well.

3 Spread cream cheese evenly over cooled baked crust. Spoon shrimp mixture over cream cheese; press lightly. Garnish with bell pepper rings and cilantro sprigs.

1 Serving: Calories 300; Total Fat 14g (Saturated Fat 7g; Trans Fat 0g); Cholesterol 85mg; Sodium 580mg; Total Carbohydrate 31g (Dietary Fiber 1g) • **Exchanges:** 1 ½ Starch, ½ Other Carbohydrate, 1 Very Lean Meat, 2 ½ Fat • **Carbohydrate Choices:** 2

Shrimp and Pancetta Pizza

Bake-Off® Contest 41, 2004   Linda Wright-Smith   Manassas, VA

Prep Time: **20 Minutes**   Start to Finish: **30 Minutes**   16 appetizers

1 package (4 oz) frozen cooked salad shrimp, thawed

1 tablespoon extra-virgin olive oil

1 clove garlic, finely chopped

1 can (13.8 oz) Pillsbury refrigerated classic pizza crust

3 oz sliced pancetta or 3 slices bacon

½ cup Alfredo pasta sauce

1 ¼ cups shredded mozzarella cheese (5 oz)

1 medium plum (Roma) tomato

3 tablespoons fresh Italian (flat-leaf) parsley leaves

1 Heat oven to 400°F. Spray cookie sheet with cooking spray. In medium bowl, mix thawed shrimp, oil and garlic until coated; set aside.

2 Unroll dough; place on sprayed cookie sheet. Starting at center, press out dough into 14×9-inch rectangle. Bake 6 to 8 minutes or until edges are light golden brown.

3 Meanwhile, in 8-inch skillet, cook pancetta over medium heat until crisp; drain on paper towels.

4 Spread Alfredo sauce over partially baked crust. Sprinkle with mozzarella cheese. Bake 6 to 10 minutes longer or until edges are golden brown and cheese is melted. Meanwhile, chop pancetta, seed and finely chop tomato; and chop parsley.

5 Top partially baked pizza evenly with shrimp, pancetta and tomato. Bake 3 minutes longer or until shrimp is thoroughly heated. Sprinkle with parsley. Cut into squares.

1 Appetizer: Calories 140; Total Fat 6g (Saturated Fat 3g; Trans Fat 0g); Cholesterol 30mg; Sodium 300mg; Total Carbohydrate 13g (Dietary Fiber 0g) • **Exchanges:** 1 Starch, ½ High-Fat Meat • **Carbohydrate Choices:** 1

Tomato-Olive-Pesto Pizza

Prep Time: **10 Minutes**   Start to Finish: **25 Minutes**   4 servings

1 can (13.8 oz) Pillsbury refrigerated classic pizza crust

⅓ cup purchased pesto

4 plum (Roma) tomatoes, thinly sliced

1 can (2 ¼ oz) sliced ripe olives, drained

¼ cup finely chopped red onion

1 ½ cups shredded Italian cheese blend (6 oz)

1 Heat oven to 425°F. Spray cookie sheet with cooking spray. Unroll dough; place on cookie sheet. Starting at center, press out dough to form 13×9-inch rectangle.

2 Spread pesto evenly over dough. Top with tomatoes, olives, onion and cheese.

3 Bake 10 to 12 minutes or until crust is deep golden brown and cheese is melted.

1 Serving: Calories 540; Total Fat 27g (Saturated Fat 10g; Trans Fat 0g); Cholesterol 35mg; Sodium 1370mg; Total Carbohydrate 53g (Dietary Fiber 2g) • **Exchanges:** 2 Starch, 1 Other Carbohydrate, 1 Vegetable, 2 High-Fat Meat, 2 Fat • **Carbohydrate Choices:** 3 ½

pizza bites Either basil pesto or sun-dried tomato pesto will make a tasty pizza.

Roasted Ratatouille Pizza

Prep Time: **35 Minutes**   Start to Finish: **45 Minutes**   4 servings

2 small Japanese eggplant,
  1-inch cubed (about 2 cups)

1 cup thinly sliced zucchini

½ cup chopped onion

4 plum (Roma) tomatoes, cut
  into ½-inch-thick slices

2 cloves garlic, finely chopped

1 tablespoon olive oil

1 teaspoon all-purpose
  seasoning mix

3 teaspoons chopped fresh
  Italian parsley

1 can (13.8 oz) Pillsbury
  refrigerated classic pizza crust

1 ½ cups shredded Swiss
  cheese (6 oz)

1   Heat oven to 425°F. In large bowl, combine eggplant, zucchini, onion, tomatoes, garlic, oil, seasoning and 2 teaspoons of the parsley; toss to coat. Arrange vegetable mixture in ungreased 15×10-inch pan. Bake on top oven rack for 10 minutes.

2   Meanwhile, lightly spray large cookie sheet with cooking spray or grease with shortening. Unroll dough; place on cookie sheet. Starting at center, press out dough to form 12×8-inch rectangle. Bake on middle oven rack 7 to 9 minutes or until light golden brown.

3   Sprinkle 1/2 cup cheese over partially baked crust. Spoon vegetable mixture over cheese. Sprinkle with remaining 1 cup cheese.

4   Bake 8 to 10 minutes longer or until crust is deep golden brown and cheese is melted. Sprinkle with remaining parsley; cut into 8 pieces.

1 Serving (2 Pieces): Calories 480; Total Fat 18g (Saturated Fat 9g; Trans Fat 0g); Cholesterol 40mg; Sodium 810mg; Total Carbohydrate 58g (Dietary Fiber 2g) • **Exchanges:** 2 ½ Starch, 1 Other Carbohydrate, 1 Vegetable, 1 ½ High-Fat Meat, 1 Fat • **Carbohydrate Choices:** 4

pizza bites Japanese eggplant is long and narrow with color that ranges from deep to light purple. The outer skin is thin and does not need to be peeled, and the flesh has a nice delicate flavor.

Bacon Spinach Pizza

Bake-Off® Contest 40, 2002   Ann Zovko   Tampa, FL

Prep: **25 Minutes**   Start to Finish: **45 Minutes**   24 servings

- 1 can (13.8 oz) Pillsbury refrigerated classic pizza crust
- 1 box (9 oz) frozen spinach in a pouch
- 1 tablespoon oil
- ½ cup coarsely chopped onion

- 1 package (6 oz) refrigerated cooked Italian-style chicken breast strips, chopped
- 2 cups shredded mozzarella cheese (8 oz)
- 1 (2.8 to 3-oz) pkg. precooked bacon slices, cut into ½-inch pieces

1 Heat oven to 400°F. Grease 15×10-inch pan with shortening or spray with cooking spray. Unroll dough; place in pan. Starting at center, press out dough to edge of pan.

2 Meanwhile, cook spinach as directed on package. Drain well; squeeze to remove liquid. Heat oil in small skillet over medium-high heat until hot. Add onion; cook and stir 3 to 4 minutes or until tender, stirring frequently.

3 Top dough with spinach, onion, chicken, cheese and bacon. Bake 18 to 20 minutes or until crust is golden brown and cheese is melted.

1 Serving: Calories 100; Total Fat 4.5g (Saturated Fat 2g; Trans Fat 0g); Cholesterol 15mg; Sodium 290mg; Total Carbohydrate 9g (Dietary Fiber 0g) • **Exchanges:** ½ Starch, 1 Lean Meat • **Carbohydrate Choices:** ½

pizza bites Cut pizza into little squares for an appetizer, or make the pizza a meal with large squares served with a crisp green salad. For a crispier crust, bake crust 9 to 13 minutes or until edges are light golden brown, then add toppings; bake pizza 9 to 12 minutes longer.

Smoky Brunch Pizza

Prep Time: **30 Minutes**   Start to Finish: **45 Minutes**   8 servings

1 can (13.8 oz) Pillsbury refrigerated classic pizza crust

2 tablespoons butter or margarine

¼ cup sliced green onions (4 medium)

¼ cup chopped red bell pepper

8 eggs

¼ cup milk

⅛ teaspoon pepper

1 package (4.5 oz) smoked salmon, flaked

½ cup reduced-fat chives-and-onion cream cheese (from 8-oz container)

1   Heat oven to 425°F. Grease 12-inch pizza pan or 13×9-inch pan with shortening or spray with cooking spray. Unroll dough; place in pan. Starting at center, press out dough to edge of pan.

2   In 10-inch skillet, melt butter over medium heat. Cook and stir onions and bell pepper in butter 2 to 3 minutes or until tender.

3   In medium bowl, beat eggs, milk and pepper. Add egg mixture to onions and bell pepper. Cook 4 to 5 minutes or until thoroughly cooked but still moist, stirring occasionally. Fold in salmon. Remove from heat. Spread cream cheese evenly over dough. Spoon cooked egg mixture over cream cheese.

4   Bake 12 to 16 minutes or until toppings are hot and crust is deep golden brown. If desired, garnish with additional green onions.

1 Serving: Calories 280; Total Fat 13g (Saturated Fat 5g; Trans Fat 0g); Cholesterol 230mg; Sodium 610mg; Total Carbohydrate 26g (Dietary Fiber 0g) • **Exchanges:** 1 ½ Starch, 1 ½ Medium-Fat Meat, 1 Fat • **Carbohydrate Choices:** 2

pizza bites For a crispier crust, bake crust 8 to 10 minutes or until crust begins to brown, then add toppings; bake pizza 9 to 12 minutes longer.

Artichoke and Red Pepper Pizza

Bake-Off® Contest 35, 1992   George Kysor   San Leandro, CA

Prep Time: **15 Minutes**   Start to Finish: **35 Minutes**   8 servings

1 can (13.8 oz) Pillsbury
refrigerated classic pizza crust

5 cloves garlic, peeled

¼ to ⅓ cup olive oil

2 red bell peppers, cut into
¼-inch strips

½ cup sliced mushrooms,
drained (from 4.5-oz jar)

3 tablespoons chopped fresh or
1 tablespoon dried basil leaves

1 jar (6 to 7 oz) marinated
artichoke hearts, drained and
chopped

1 can (2 ¼ oz) sliced ripe
olives, drained

2 cups shredded mozzarella
cheese (8 oz)

½ cup grated Parmesan cheese

1 Heat oven to 425°F. Grease 13×9-inch (3-quart) baking dish or 12-inch pizza pan with shortening or spray with cooking spray. Unroll dough; place in pan. Starting at center, press out dough to edge of pan.

2 In food processor or blender, process garlic 10 to 15 seconds or until finely chopped. Reserve 1 tablespoon of the oil. With machine running, add remaining oil all at once through feed tube or opening in blender lid. Process 20 to 30 seconds or just until blended.

3 Spread garlic mixture over dough. Heat reserved 1 tablespoon oil in medium skillet over medium-high heat until hot; cook and stir peppers in oil until crisp-tender, 3 to 5 minutes. Layer peppers, mushrooms, basil, artichokes and olives over garlic mixture; top with cheeses.

4 Bake 14 to 18 minutes until crust is golden brown around edges and cheese is melted.

1 Serving: Calories 330; Total Fat 17g (Saturated Fat 6g; Trans Fat 0g); Cholesterol 20mg; Sodium 730mg; Total Carbohydrate 29g (Dietary Fiber 2g) • **Exchanges:** 1 Starch, 1 Other Carbohydrate, 1 ½ High-Fat Meat, 1 Fat • **Carbohydrate Choices:** 2

Caribbean Black Bean Pizza

Prep Time: **15 Minutes**   Start to Finish: **30 Minutes**   6 servings

1 can (13.8 oz) Pillsbury refrigerated classic pizza crust

1 can (8 oz) no-salt-added tomato sauce

2 cans (15 oz each) black beans, drained, rinsed

1 can (8 oz) pineapple tidbits in juice, well drained

½ fresh lime or 4 teaspoons lime juice

2 tablespoons chopped fresh cilantro

1 ½ cups shredded mozzarella cheese (6 oz)

1   Heat oven to 425°F. Spray 15×10-inch pan with cooking spray. Unroll dough; place in pan. Starting at center, press out dough to edge and up sides of pan. Bake 5 minutes.

2   Spread tomato sauce evenly over partially baked crust. Top with beans and pineapple. Squeeze lime juice over toppings. Top with cilantro and cheese.

3   Bake 11 to 14 minutes longer or until bottom of crust is deep golden brown.

1 Serving: Calories 450; Total Fat 9g (Saturated Fat 4g; Trans Fat 0g); Cholesterol 15mg; Sodium 630mg; Total Carbohydrate 71g (Dietary Fiber 13g) • **Exchanges:** 3 Starch, 1 ½ Other Carbohydrate, 2 Very Lean Meat, 1 Fat • **Carbohydrate Choices:** 5

pizza bites 1 cup (4 ounces) chopped smoked turkey breast can be substituted for 1 can of the beans.

3 Pizza in Disguise

Easy Stromboli

Prep Time: **15 Minutes**   Start to Finish: **35 Minutes**   6 servings

½ lb lean (at least 80%) ground beef	1 cup shredded mozzarella cheese (4 oz)
1 can (13.8 oz) Pillsbury refrigerated classic pizza crust	¼ cup chopped green and/or red bell pepper, if desired
¼ cup pizza sauce	¼ teaspoon Italian seasoning

1 Heat oven to 400°F. Spray cookie sheet with cooking spray. In 8-inch skillet, cook beef over medium-high heat until thoroughly cooked, stirring frequently. Drain and set aside.

2 Unroll dough; place on cookie sheet. Starting at center, press out dough to form 12×8-inch rectangle. Spread sauce over dough to within 2 inches of long sides and 1/2 inch of short sides. Place beef lengthwise down center, forming 3-inch-wide strip and to within 1/2 inch of short sides. Top with cheese, bell pepper and Italian seasoning. Fold long sides of dough over filling; press edges to seal.

3 Bake 15 to 20 minutes or until crust is golden brown.

1 Serving: Calories 290; Total Fat 10g (Saturated Fat 4.5g; Trans Fat 0g); Cholesterol 35mg; Sodium 630mg; Total Carbohydrate 33g (Dietary Fiber 0g) • **Exchanges:** 1 Starch, 1 Other Carbohydrate, 2 Medium-Fat Meat • **Carbohydrate Choices:** 2

pizza bites For a flavor change, use 1/2 pound bulk Italian sausage, cooked and drained, for the ground beef.

Breakfast Calzones

Prep Time: **15 Minutes**   Start to Finish: **30 Minutes**   4 calzones

4 eggs

¼ cup milk

Dash pepper

2 teaspoons margarine or butter

1 can (13.8 oz) Pillsbury refrigerated classic pizza crust

½ cup shredded mozzarella cheese (2 oz)

16 slices pepperoni (from 3.5-oz package) pepperoni

4 teaspoons grated Parmesan cheese

1 Heat oven to 400°F. Spray large cookie sheet with cooking spray. In medium bowl, combine eggs, milk and pepper; beat until well blended. In medium nonstick skillet, melt margarine over medium heat. Add egg mixture; cook 3 to 5 minutes or until eggs are set but moist, stirring occasionally.

2 Unroll dough; place on work surface. Starting at center, press out dough to form 14×10-inch rectangle. Cut dough into four 7×5-inch rectangles. Divide mozzarella cheese evenly onto half of each rectangle to within 1/2 inch of edges. Top cheese with pepperoni, Parmesan cheese and eggs. Fold untopped dough over filling, turnover fashion; press edges firmly to seal. Place on sprayed cookie sheet.

3 Bake at 400°F for 11 to 13 minutes or until golden brown.

1 Calzone: Calories 500; Total Fat 23g (Saturated Fat 9g; Trans Fat 1g); Cholesterol 250mg; Sodium 1300mg; Total Carbohydrate 49g (Dietary Fiber 0g) • **Exchanges:** 2 Starch, 1 Other Carbohydrate, 2 ½ Medium-Fat Meat, 2 Fat • **Carbohydrate Choices:** 3

Garden Vegetable Calzones

Prep Time: **20 Minutes**   Start to Finish: **35 Minutes**   4 calzones

¾ cup sliced fresh mushrooms (about 2 oz)

1 small zucchini, cut in half lengthwise, thinly sliced (¾ cup)

½ cup coarsely chopped red or yellow bell pepper

¼ cup sliced green onions (4 medium)

¼ teaspoon garlic salt

¼ teaspoon dried basil leaves

1 can (13.8 oz) Pillsbury refrigerated classic pizza crust

4 oz shredded mozzarella or provolone cheese (1 cup)

1 egg white, beaten

1 Heat oven to 425°F. Spray cookie sheet with cooking spray. In medium bowl, combine mushrooms, zucchini, bell pepper and onions. Sprinkle with garlic salt and basil; mix well.

2 Unroll dough; place on cookie sheet. Starting at center, press out dough to form 14-inch square; cut into four 7-inch squares. Place 1/4 cup cheese on half of each square; spread to within 1/2 inch of edge. Top each with 1/4 of vegetable mixture.

3 Fold dough in half over filling; press edges firmly with fork to seal. Brush each with beaten egg white. With sharp knife, cut 2 or 3 slits in top of each for steam to escape.

4 Bake 12 to 15 minutes or until golden brown.

1 Calzone: Calories 350; Total Fat 9g (Saturated Fat 4.5g; Trans Fat 0g); Cholesterol 15mg; Sodium 930mg; Total Carbohydrate 51g (Dietary Fiber 0g) • **Exchanges:** 1 ½ Starch, 1 ½ Other Carbohydrate, 1 Vegetable, 1 ½ Medium-Fat Meat • **Carbohydrate Choices:** 3 ½

pizza bites Calzones are portable and easy to reheat in the microwave. Place one calzone on a microwave-safe paper towel and microwave on Medium for 1 to 1 1/2 minutes or until the cheese is melted and calzone is hot, turning once halfway through cooking.

Chocolate-Hazelnut Breakfast Ring

Prep Time: **20 Minutes**   Start to Finish: **55 Minutes**   8 servings

1 can (13.8 oz) Pillsbury refrigerated classic pizza crust

⅔ cup hazelnut spread with cocoa (from 13-oz jar), stirred to soften

½ cup whole hazelnuts (filberts), toasted,* finely chopped

1 egg, beaten

½ teaspoon granulated sugar

1 teaspoon powdered sugar

1 Heat oven to 350°F. Line cookie sheet with cooking parchment paper. On lightly floured work surface, unroll dough; starting at center, press out dough to form 13×10-inch rectangle. Gently spread hazelnut spread to within 1/2 inch of edges. Sprinkle with toasted hazelnuts.

2 Fold long sides of dough over filling to meet in center. Starting with 1 long side, loosely roll up dough. Shape dough roll into ring on cookie sheet; pinch ends together to seal. Cut 5 (1-inch-deep) slits in top of dough. Brush with beaten egg; sprinkle with granulated sugar.

3 Bake 20 to 25 minutes or until golden brown. Remove from cookie sheet; place on serving platter. Cool 10 minutes before serving. Sprinkle with powdered sugar; serve warm.

1 Serving: Calories 310; Total Fat 14g (Saturated Fat 2g; Trans Fat 0g); Cholesterol 25mg; Sodium 370mg; Total Carbohydrate 40g (Dietary Fiber 2g) • **Exchanges:** 1 Starch, 1 ½ Other Carbohydrate, ½ High-Fat Meat, 2 Fat • **Carbohydrate Choices:** 2 ½

*To toast whole hazelnuts, spread them on a cookie sheet and bake at 375°F for 5 to 8 minutes or until golden brown. To remove the skins, roll the warm nuts in a clean kitchen towel.

Pepperoni Calzones

Prep Time: **20 Minutes**   Start to Finish: **35 Minutes**   6 servings

1 can (13.8 oz) Pillsbury refrigerated classic pizza crust

6 tablespoons pizza sauce

36 pepperoni slices (from 3.5-oz package)

⅓ cup chopped onion

⅓ cup chopped green bell pepper

1 ¼ cups shredded mozzarella cheese (5 oz)

Additional pizza sauce

1 Heat oven to 425°F. Grease cookie sheet with shortening.

2 Unroll dough; place on cookie sheet. Starting at center, press out dough to form 14×12-inch rectangle. Cut into 6 equal rectangles.

3 Spread each rectangle with 1 tablespoon pizza sauce to within 1/2 inch of edges. Place 6 pepperoni slices on longest side of each rectangle. Top with onion, bell pepper and 1 cup of the cheese. Starting with longest side, fold dough over pepperoni mixture. Seal edges with a fork. Cut 3 (2-inch) slits in top of each rectangle.

4 Bake 9 to 13 minutes or until light golden brown. Remove from oven; sprinkle evenly with remaining 1/4 cup cheese. Bake 1 to 2 minutes longer or until cheese is melted. Serve with additional pizza sauce, if desired.

1 Serving: Calories 400; Total Fat 20g (Saturated Fat 9g; Trans Fat 0g); Cholesterol 50mg; Sodium 1250mg; Total Carbohydrate 36g (Dietary Fiber 1g) • **Exchanges:** 1 Starch, 1 ½ Other Carbohydrate, 2 High-Fat Meat, ½ Fat • **Carbohydrate Choices:** 2 ½

Ham and Cheese Calzones

Prep Time: **10 Minutes**   Start to Finish: **30 Minutes**   4 calzones

½ **cup shredded Cheddar cheese (2 oz)**

½ **cup shredded Swiss cheese (2 oz)**

1 **cup chopped cooked ham**

¼ **cup chopped green or red bell pepper**

½ **teaspoon dried basil leaves**

1 **can (13.8 oz) Pillsbury refrigerated classic pizza crust**

1   Heat oven to 425°F. Grease cookie sheet with shortening. In medium bowl, combine all ingredients except pizza crust; mix well.

2   Unroll dough; place on cookie sheet. Starting at center, press out dough to form 14×8-inch rectangle. Cut into four 7×4-inch rectangles; separate slightly.

3   Spoon about 1/2 cup ham and cheese mixture onto half of each rectangle; fold dough over filling. Press edges with fork to seal; prick tops with fork.

4   Bake 11 to 16 minutes or until golden brown.

1 Calzone: Calories 410; Total Fat 15g (Saturated Fat 7g; Trans Fat 0g); Cholesterol 50mg; Sodium 1320mg; Total Carbohydrate 48g (Dietary Fiber 0g) • **Exchanges:** 2 Starch, 1 Other Carbohydrate, 2 ½ Medium-Fat Meat • **Carbohydrate Choices:** 3

Braided Stuffed Pizza Bread

Bake-Off® Contest 35, 1992   Elisabeth Williams   North Andover, MA

Prep Time: **15 Minutes**   Start to Finish: **35 Minutes**   12 servings

1 can (13.8 oz) Pillsbury refrigerated classic pizza crust

2 tablespoons Boursin cheese with garlic and herbs

3 oz thinly sliced Canadian bacon

10 slices pepperoni (from 3.5-oz package)

1 cup shredded mozzarella cheese (4 oz)

2 tablespoons shredded Parmesan cheese

1 egg yolk

1 teaspoon water

1 to 2 teaspoons poppy seed

Pizza sauce, if desired

1   Heat oven to 400°F. Spray cookie sheet with cooking spray. Unroll dough; place on cookie sheet. Starting at center, press out dough to form 14×11-inch rectangle.

2   Spread garlic and herb cheese lengthwise down center 1/3 of rectangle to within 1/2 inch of short ends. Top with Canadian bacon, pepperoni, mozzarella and Parmesan cheese.

3   With scissors or sharp knife, make cuts 1 inch apart on long sides of dough to within 1/2 inch of filling. Alternately cross strips over filling. Fold ends under to seal.

4   In small bowl, mix egg yolk and water until well blended. Brush over dough; sprinkle with poppy seed.

5   Bake 11 to 16 minutes or until golden brown. Cut into crosswise slices. Serve with pizza sauce.

1 Serving: Calories 160; Total Fat 7g (Saturated Fat 3g; Trans Fat 0g); Cholesterol 35mg; Sodium 500mg; Total Carbohydrate 16g (Dietary Fiber 0g) • **Exchanges:** ½ Starch, ½ Other Carbohydrate, 1 High-Fat Meat • **Carbohydrate Choices:** 1

pizza bites Try hot and spicy pepperoni to fire up this pizza snack.

Pizza Calzone

Prep Time: **20 Minutes**   Start to Finish: **55 Minutes**   8 servings

2 cans (13.8 oz each) Pillsbury refrigerated classic pizza crust

42 slices pepperoni (from 3.5-oz package)

1 jar (4.5 oz) sliced mushrooms, well drained

½ cup sliced pimiento-stuffed green olives

8 oz thinly sliced provolone cheese

1 tablespoon grated Parmesan cheese

1 jar (14 oz) pizza sauce, heated

1 Heat oven to 375°F. Lightly grease 12-inch pizza pan with shortening. Unroll 1 can of dough; place in pan. Starting at center, press out dough to edge of pan. Layer pepperoni, mushrooms, olives and provolone cheese over dough.

2 Unroll remaining can of dough. Press out dough on work surface to form 12-inch round. Fold dough in half; place over provolone cheese and unfold. Press outside edges to seal. Cut several slits in top crust for steam to escape. Sprinkle with Parmesan cheese.

3 Bake 30 to 35 minutes or until crust is deep golden brown. Cut pizza into wedges; serve with warm pizza sauce.

1 Serving: Calories 430; Total Fat 17g (Saturated Fat 8g; Trans Fat 0g); Cholesterol 35mg; Sodium 1590mg; Total Carbohydrate 53g (Dietary Fiber 1g) • **Exchanges:** 2 ½ Starch, 1 Other Carbohydrate, 1 ½ High-Fat Meat, ½ Fat • **Carbohydrate Choices:** 3 ½

pizza bites Vary the calzone filling with your favorite pizza ingredients. Try an all-veggie version with chopped broccoli, bell peppers and onion with shredded mozzarella and Parmesan cheeses.

Pizza Dogs

Prep Time: **15 Minutes**   Start to Finish: **25 Minutes**   6 servings

6 hot dogs

3 slices (¾ oz each) American cheese, each cut into 4 strips

1 can (13.8 oz) **Pillsbury refrigerated classic pizza crust**

¾ cup tomato pasta sauce, heated

1 Heat oven to 425°F. Spray cookie sheet with cooking spray. Cut slit in each hot dog lengthwise to within 1/2 inch of each end. Place 2 cheese strips in each slit.

2 Unroll dough; place on work surface. Starting at center, press out dough to form 12×8-inch rectangle. Cut dough crosswise in half; cut each half crosswise into 3 rectangles, each about 6×2 1/2 inches.

3 Place 1 hot dog, cheese side down, in center of each dough rectangle. Wrap dough around hot dogs, covering completely and pinching sides and ends to seal. Place seam side down on cookie sheet.

4 Bake 6 to 9 minutes or until light golden brown. Serve with warm pasta sauce for dipping.

1 Serving: Calories 380; Total Fat 19g (Saturated Fat 8g; Trans Fat 0g); Cholesterol 35mg; Sodium 1310mg; Total Carbohydrate 39g (Dietary Fiber 0g) • **Exchanges:** 1 ½ Starch, 1 Other Carbohydrate, 1 High-Fat Meat, 2 Fat • **Carbohydrate Choices:** 2 ½

pizza bites For a shiny golden brown crust, brush wrapped hot dogs with beaten egg white after placing on cookie sheet.

Chicken-Cheese Baked Pizza Sandwich

Prep Time: **15 Minutes**   Start to Finish: **45 Minutes**   8 servings

1 tablespoon butter or margarine

1 medium onion, halved, thinly sliced

1 medium bell pepper (any color), cut into thin strips

2 cans (13.8 oz each) Pillsbury refrigerated classic pizza crust

2 tablespoons creamy Dijon mustard-mayonnaise spread

½ lb thinly sliced cooked chicken

40 slices pepperoni (from 3.5-oz package)

8 oz thinly sliced Cheddar cheese or mozzarella

1 egg

1 teaspoon sesame seed

1 Heat oven to 400°F. Grease 13×9-inch pan with shortening or spray with cooking spray. In 10-inch skillet, melt butter over medium-high heat. Add onion and bell pepper; cook 3 to 5 minutes, stirring occasionally, until tender.

2 Unroll 1 can of the dough; place in pan. Starting at center, press out dough just to edge of pan (do not go up sides). Spread mustard-mayonnaise over dough. Top evenly with chicken, pepperoni, onion mixture and cheese.

3 Unroll remaining can of dough over cheese, stretching to edges. In small bowl, beat egg; brush over top. Sprinkle with sesame seed.

4 Bake 23 to 28 minutes or until golden brown and thoroughly heated. Let stand 10 minutes. Cut into 8 pieces to serve.

1 Serving: Calories 500; Total Fat 21g (Saturated Fat 10g; Trans Fat 0g); Cholesterol 100mg; Sodium 1170mg; Total Carbohydrate 50g (Dietary Fiber 0g) • **Exchanges:** 2 Starch, 1 ½ Other Carbohydrate, 3 Lean Meat, 2 Fat • **Carbohydrate Choices:** 3

Hot Pepper-Chicken Sandwich Slices

Bake-Off® Contest 39, 2000   Leo Maron   Springfield, MA

Prep Time: **15 Minutes**   Start to Finish: **40 Minutes**   10 servings

1 cup cubed hot pepper Monterey Jack cheese (4 oz)

¼ cup chopped drained roasted red bell peppers (from 7.25-oz jar)

4 ½ teaspoons chopped ripe olives

1 shallot, minced

1 can (5 oz) chunk chicken in water, drained

Dash salt

Dash pepper

1 can (13.8 oz) Pillsbury refrigerated classic pizza crust

1 egg

1 tablespoon water

1 Heat oven to 375°F. In medium bowl, combine cheese, roasted peppers, olives, shallot, chicken, salt and pepper; mix well. Set aside.

2 Unroll dough; place on ungreased cookie sheet. Starting at center, press out dough to form 14×9-inch rectangle. In small bowl, combine egg and water; beat well. Brush lightly over dough.

3 Spoon cheese mixture lengthwise in 3-inch-wide strip down center of dough to within 1/4 inch of each end. Bring long sides of dough up over cheese until edges touch. Press ends to seal. Brush lightly with egg mixture.

4 Bake 20 to 25 minutes or until deep golden brown. Cut into crosswise slices.

1 Serving: Calories 160; Total Fat 5g (Saturated Fat 2.5g; Trans Fat 0g); Cholesterol 35mg; Sodium 420mg; Total Carbohydrate 19g (Dietary Fiber 0g) • **Exchanges:** 1 Starch, ½ Other Carbohydrate, 1 Lean Meat • **Carbohydrate Choices:** 1

Italian Chicken Salad Panini

Prep Time: **30 Minutes**   Start to Finish: **30 Minutes**   4 sandwiches

1 can (13.8 oz) Pillsbury refrigerated classic pizza crust

1 teaspoon olive oil

½ teaspoon Italian seasoning

1 package (6 oz) refrigerated cooked Italian-style chicken breast strips, finely chopped

2 tablespoons finely chopped green onions (2 medium)

3 tablespoons mayonnaise or salad dressing

1 large tomato, thinly sliced

4 slices (about 1 oz each) Jarlsberg cheese (from deli)

1 Heat oven to 400°F. Grease large cookie sheet with shortening or cooking spray. Unroll dough onto cookie sheet. Starting at center, press out dough into 15×10-inch rectangle. Brush oil over dough. Sprinkle evenly with Italian seasoning.

2 Bake 10 to 13 minutes or until edges are golden brown. Meanwhile, in medium bowl, mix chicken, onions and mayonnaise.

3 Cut baked crust in half crosswise. Spread chicken mixture on 1 half. Top with tomato and cheese, cutting to fit if necessary. Cover with remaining half of baked crust, seasoning side down. Cut into 4 sandwiches.

4 Heat 12-inch skillet over medium-low heat. Place 2 sandwiches in skillet; cook about 2 minutes, pressing down with pancake turner, until bottom crust is deep golden brown. Turn sandwiches; cook about 2 minutes, pressing again with turner, until cheese is melted. Repeat with remaining 2 sandwiches.

1 Sandwich: Calories 525; Total Fat 23g (Saturated Fat 7g, Trans Fat 0); Cholesterol 70mg; Sodium 1010mg; Total Carbohydrate 50g (Dietary Fiber 1g) • **Exchanges:** 3 Starch, 3 Lean Meat, 2 1/2 Fat • **Carbohydrate Choices:** 3

Chicken Salad Focaccia Sandwiches

Bake-Off® Contest 38, 1998   Westy Gabany   Olney, MD

Prep Time: **30 Minutes**   Start to Finish: **30 Minutes**   4 sandwiches

Focaccia

1 can (13.8 oz) Pillsbury refrigerated classic pizza crust

2 to 3 tablespoons olive oil

2 cloves garlic, finely chopped

½ to 1 ½ teaspoons kosher (coarse) salt

1 ½ teaspoons dried rosemary leaves

Salad

1 ⅓ cups chopped cooked chicken

½ cup chopped celery

½ cup mayonnaise or salad dressing

2 medium green onions, chopped (1 tablespoon)

1 teaspoon dried tarragon leaves

½ teaspoon yellow mustard

Dash garlic powder

Dash onion powder

1 Heat oven to 350°F. Lightly spray cookie sheet with cooking spray. Unroll dough; place on cookie sheet. Starting at center, press out dough to form 12×10-inch rectangle. Starting with short end, fold dough in half; press lightly.

2 In small bowl, mix oil and chopped garlic. Spread over dough. Sprinkle with salt and rosemary. Bake 20 to 25 minutes or until edges are golden brown.

3 In medium bowl, mix salad ingredients. Refrigerate 15 minutes. Cut warm focaccia into 4 pieces. Split each piece to make 2 layers. Spread salad on bottom halves; cover with top halves.

1 Sandwich: Calories 560; Total Fat 32g (Saturated Fat 5g; Trans Fat 0g); Cholesterol 35mg; Sodium 1370mg; Total Carbohydrate 50g (Dietary Fiber 0g) • **Exchanges:** 2 Starch, 1 ½ Other Carbohydrate, 1 ½ Lean Meat, 5 Fat • **Carbohydrate Choices:** 3

Easy Beef Focaccia Sandwiches

Prep Time: **35 Minutes**   Start to Finish: **35 Minutes**   4 sandwiches

Focaccia Crust

1 can (13.8 oz) Pillsbury refrigerated classic pizza crust

1 tablespoon olive oil

½ teaspoon garlic powder

½ teaspoon dried basil leaves

Filling

¼ cup mayonnaise

2 tablespoons creamy horseradish sauce

4 slices (1 oz each) provolone cheese

½ lb sliced cooked roast beef (from deli)

2 medium tomatoes, thinly sliced (1 ½ cups)

1 cup shredded romaine lettuce

1 Heat oven to 375°F. Spray 15×10-inch pan with cooking spray. Unroll dough; place in pan. Starting at center, press out dough to edge of pan. Brush with oil; sprinkle with garlic powder and basil. Bake 10 minutes or until golden brown. Cool 15 minutes.

2 Meanwhile, in small bowl, mix mayonnaise and horseradish sauce until well blended.

3 Cut focaccia crust into 8 rectangles. Spread mayonnaise mixture on bottom sides of all rectangles. On 4 rectangles, layer cheese, beef, tomatoes and lettuce over mayonnaise mixture. Cover with remaining rectangles, mayonnaise mixture side down. Cut each sandwich in half.

1 Sandwich: Calories 600; Total Fat 28g (Saturated Fat 9g; Trans Fat 0g); Cholesterol 75mg; Sodium 1080mg; Total Carbohydrate 52g (Dietary Fiber 1g) • **Exchanges:** 2 Starch, 1 ½ Other Carbohydrate, 4 Lean Meat, 3 Fat • **Carbohydrate Choices:** 3 ½

pizza bites For a flavor change, use sliced ham or turkey in place of the beef, and Swiss or Cheddar cheese in place of the provolone.

Beef and Vegetable Foldover

Prep Time: **30 Minutes** Start to Finish: **55 Minutes** 4 servings

1 jar (12 oz) homestyle beef
gravy

2 tablespoons chili sauce

1/4 teaspoon dried marjoram
leaves

3/4 lb lean boneless beef sirloin
steak, cut into 1/2-inch cubes

1/2 cup chopped onion

1/8 teaspoon pepper

1 cup frozen southern-style
hash-brown potatoes

1 cup frozen mixed vegetables

1 can (13.8 oz) Pillsbury
refrigerated classic pizza crust

1 egg

1 tablespoon water

1 Heat oven to 400°F. Line 15×10-inch baking pan with foil. Spray foil
with cooking spray. In small saucepan, combine gravy, chili sauce and
marjoram; mix well. Set aside.

2 Spray large skillet with cooking spray. Heat over medium-high heat
until hot. Add beef, onion and pepper; cook and stir 4 to 6 minutes
or until beef is browned. Add hash-brown potatoes and mixed
vegetables; mix well. Add 1/4 cup of the gravy mixture; cook and stir
1 minute. Remove skillet from heat.

3 Unroll dough; place in foil-lined pan. Starting at center, press out
dough to form 14×9-inch rectangle. Spread beef mixture lengthwise
on half of dough. Fold other half of dough over filling; press edges
with fork to seal. Cut 4 small slits down center of top of dough. In
small bowl, beat egg and water. Brush over top of dough.

4 Bake 20 to 25 minutes or until deep golden brown. Meanwhile, heat
gravy mixture over low heat until hot. Serve foldover with warm
gravy.

1 Serving: Calories 500; Total Fat 9g (Saturated Fat 3g; Trans Fat 0g); Cholesterol 105mg;
Sodium 1360mg; Total Carbohydrate 71g (Dietary Fiber 4g) • **Exchanges:** 3 Starch, 1 1/2
Other Carbohydrate, 3 1/2 Very Lean Meat, 1 Fat • **Carbohydrate Choices:** 5

Deep-Dish Pizza Pie Bundle

Prep Time: **10 Minutes**   Start to Finish: **35 Minutes**   4 servings

1 can (13.8 oz) Pillsbury refrigerated classic pizza crust

2 cups shredded mozzarella cheese (8 oz)

⅓ cup pizza sauce

25 slices pepperoni (from 3.5-oz package)

1 tablespoon grated Parmesan cheese

1 Heat oven to 400°F. Spray 8-inch round cake pan with cooking spray. Unroll dough; place on work surface. Starting at center, press out dough to form 14×10-inch rectangle. Place in pan with sides of dough extending evenly over sides of pan. Lightly press dough in bottom and up sides of pan.

2 Sprinkle 1 cup of the mozzarella cheese over dough. Spread pizza sauce evenly over cheese. Top with pepperoni and remaining 1 cup mozzarella cheese.

3 With scissors, make 2-inch cut into each corner of dough. Bring all ends of dough together at center; twist to secure at top of pizza. Sprinkle with Parmesan cheese.

4 Bake 20 to 25 minutes or until deep golden brown.

1 Serving: Calories 480; Total Fat 20g (Saturated Fat 10g; Trans Fat 0g); Cholesterol 45mg; Sodium 1340mg; Total Carbohydrate 51g (Dietary Fiber 0g) • **Exchanges:** 2 ½ Starch, 1 Other Carbohydrate, 2 ½ Medium-Fat Meat, 1 Fat • **Carbohydrate Choices:** 3 ½

4

Pizza Snacks, Appetizers & Desserts

Pizza Dipping Sticks

Prep Time: **10 Minutes**   Start to Finish: **25 Minutes**   4 servings

1 can (13.8 oz) Pillsbury refrigerated classic pizza crust

1 ½ cups shredded mozzarella cheese (6 oz)

30 slices pepperoni (from 3.5-oz package)

1 to 1 ½ cups pizza sauce, warmed

1 Heat oven to 400°F. Grease cookie sheet with shortening, or spray with cooking spray. Unroll dough; place on cookie sheet. Starting at center, press out dough into 13×9-inch rectangle. Bake 7 minutes.

2 Top partially baked crust with pepperoni and cheese.

3 Bake 8 to 10 minutes longer or until cheese is melted. Cool 2 minutes. Cut pizza in half lengthwise, then cut into 16 (1 1/2 inch) strips. Serve with pizza sauce for dipping.

1 Serving (4 Strips): Calories 580; Total Fat 28g (Saturated Fat 13g; Trans Fat 0g); Cholesterol 70mg; Sodium 1940mg; Total Carbohydrate 55g (Dietary Fiber 1g) • **Exchanges:** 2 ½ Starch, 1 Other Carbohydrate, 3 High-Fat Meat, ½ Fat • **Carbohydrate Choices:** 3 ½

Peppy Pizza Dip with Crisp Italian Pizza Wedges

Prep Time: **30 Minutes**   Start to Finish: **30 Minutes**   16 servings

Focaccia Wedges

2 cans (13.8 oz each) Pillsbury refrigerated classic pizza crust

2 tablespoons olive oil

2 teaspoons dried Italian seasoning

2 teaspoons finely chopped garlic (about 4 medium cloves) garlic

½ cup shredded or grated Parmesan cheese (2 oz)

Pizza Dip

¾ cup pizza sauce

¾ cup chopped pepperoni (2 ½ oz)

1 cup shredded mozzarella cheese (4 oz)

1 tablespoon shredded or grated Parmesan cheese

1 tablespoon chopped onion

1 tablespoon chopped green bell pepper

½ teaspoon dried basil leaves

½ teaspoon dried oregano leaves

1 clove garlic, finely chopped

1 Heat oven to 425°F. Lightly grease 2 cookie sheets with shortening. Unroll dough from each can; place on cookie sheets. Starting at centers, press out dough to form two 12×8-inch rectangles. Using fingers, press indentations randomly over dough. Brush each rectangle with olive oil. Sprinkle each with Italian seasoning, 1 teaspoon garlic and 1/4 cup Parmesan cheese. Bake 10 to 12 minutes or until golden brown.

2 Meanwhile, in microwave-safe bowl, combine all pizza dip ingredients; mix well. Microwave on High for 3 minutes. Stir well; microwave on High for an additional 2 minutes or until cheese is melted. Stir.

3 Cut warm pizza into triangles. Serve with warm pizza dip.

1 Serving: Calories 200; Total Fat 8g (Saturated Fat 3g; Trans Fat 0g); Cholesterol 10mg; Sodium 590mg; Total Carbohydrate 25g (Dietary Fiber 0g) • **Exchanges:** 1 Starch, ½ Other Carbohydrate, ½ High-Fat Meat, 1 Fat • **Carbohydrate Choices:** 1 ½

Red Bell Pepper and Olive Pizza Sticks

Prep Time: **15 Minutes**   Start to Finish: **30 Minutes**   28 servings

1 can (13.8 oz) Pillsbury refrigerated classic pizza crust

1 tablespoon extra-virgin olive oil

1/3 cup red bell pepper strips (1 × 1/8 inch)

3 tablespoons thinly slivered pitted ripe olives

1 tablespoon chopped fresh rosemary

1/4 teaspoon kosher (coarse) salt

1 cup tomato pasta sauce, heated

1 Heat oven to 400°F. Grease cookie sheet with shortening or spray with cooking spray. Unroll dough; place on cookie sheet. Starting from center, press out dough to form 14×9-inch rectangle. With fingertips, make indentations over surface of dough.

2 Drizzle oil over dough. Top with remaining ingredients except pasta sauce; press lightly into dough.

3 Bake 13 to 18 minutes or until golden brown. Cut pizza in half lengthwise; cut each half crosswise into 14 sticks. Serve warm sticks with warm pasta sauce for dipping.

1 Serving: Calories 50; Total Fat 1.5g (Saturated Fat 0g; Trans Fat 0g); Cholesterol 0mg; Sodium 170mg; Total Carbohydrate 8g (Dietary Fiber 0g) • **Exchanges:** 1/2 Starch • **Carbohydrate Choices:** 1/2

pizza bites Use your hands to press the toppings gently into the dough so they don't fall off when you cut the sticks.

Marinara and Shrimp Mini Pizzas

Prep Time: **15 Minutes**   Start to Finish: **30 Minutes**   16 pizzas

1 can (13.8 oz) Pillsbury refrigerated classic pizza crust

⅓ cup refrigerated marinara sauce

⅓ cup chopped packaged precooked bacon

16 cooked deveined peeled medium shrimp, thawed if frozen, tail shells removed

2 tablespoons shredded Parmesan cheese

Chopped fresh chives, if desired

1 Heat oven to 425°F. Spray cookie sheet with cooking spray. Unroll dough; place on work surface. Starting at center, press out dough to form 12×8-inch rectangle. With floured 2-inch cookie cutters, cut dough into shapes. On cookie sheet, place shapes 1 inch apart. Bake 5 to 7 minutes or until light golden brown.

2 Spread marinara sauce evenly over each partially baked crust. Sprinkle bacon evenly over each crust. Place shrimp in center of each. Sprinkle each with cheese.

3 Bake 3 to 5 minutes longer or until cheese is melted; sprinkle with chives.

1 Pizza: Calories 80; Total Fat 2g (Saturated Fat 0.5g; Trans Fat 0g); Cholesterol 10mg; Sodium 250mg; Total Carbohydrate 13g (Dietary Fiber 0g) • **Exchanges:** 1 Starch • **Carbohydrate Choices:** 1

pizza bites Just before baking these mini pizzas, sprinkle them with chopped fresh basil or parsley.

Stuffed-Crust Pizza Snacks

Bake-Off® Contest 39, 2000   Ellen Hyde   Culpeper, VA

Prep Time: **20 Minutes**   Start to Finish: **45 Minutes**   48 appetizers

2 cans (13.8 oz each) Pillsbury refrigerated classic pizza crust	1 ½ teaspoons dried Italian seasoning
8 oz mozzarella cheese, cut into 48 cubes	2 tablespoons grated Parmesan cheese
48 slices pepperoni (from 3.5-oz package)	1 jar (14 oz) pizza sauce, heated
¼ cup olive or vegetable oil	

1 Heat oven to 400°F. Spray two 9-inch pie pans or one 13×9-inch pan with cooking spray. Remove dough from both cans. Unroll dough; place in pans. Starting at center, press out each dough rectangle to form 12×8-inch rectangle. Cut each rectangle into 24 squares.

2 Top each square with cheese cube and pepperoni slice. Wrap dough around filling to completely cover; firmly press edges to seal. Place seam side down with sides touching in sprayed pie pans.

3 In small bowl, combine oil and Italian seasoning; mix well. Drizzle over filled dough in pans. Sprinkle with Parmesan cheese.

4 Bake 16 to 22 minutes or until golden brown. Serve warm pizza bites with warm pizza sauce.

1 Appetizer: Calories 80; Total Fat 3.5g (Saturated Fat 1g; Trans Fat 0g); Cholesterol 0mg; Sodium 220mg; Total Carbohydrate 9g (Dietary Fiber 0g) • **Exchanges:** ½ Starch, ½ High-Fat Meat • **Carbohydrate Choices:** ½

Mini Pizzas

Prep Time: **20 Minutes**   Start to Finish: **25 Minutes**   20 pizzas

1 can (13.8 oz) Pillsbury refrigerated classic pizza crust	20 slices plum (Roma) tomatoes
⅓ cup basil pesto	1 cup shredded mozzarella cheese (4 oz)

1 Heat oven to 425°F. Lightly grease cookie sheet with shortening. Unroll dough; place on work surface. Starting at center, press out dough to form 12×8-inch rectangle. With round cutter, cut dough into rounds; place 1 inch apart on greased cookie sheet.

2 Bake 5 to 7 minutes or until light golden brown.

3 Spread pesto evenly over each partially baked crust. Top each with 1 tomato slice. Sprinkle with cheese.

4 Bake 3 to 5 minutes longer or until cheese is melted.

1 Pizza: Calories 90; Total Fat 4g (Saturated Fat 1.5g; Trans Fat 0g); Cholesterol 0mg; Sodium 210mg; Total Carbohydrate 11g (Dietary Fiber 0g) • **Exchanges:** ½ Starch, ½ High-Fat Meat • **Carbohydrate Choices:** 1

pizza bites Serve mini pizzas with a variety of your favorite pizza toppings, such as cooked Italian sausage, pepperoni, chopped cooked chicken, chopped or sliced fresh veggies and shredded cheeses.

Zesty Cheese Bread

Bake-Off® Contest 38, 1998   Barbara Jones   Norristown, PA

Prep Time: **10 Minutes**   Start to Finish: **45 Minutes**   10 servings

- 1 can (13.8 oz) Pillsbury refrigerated classic pizza crust
- 1 can (4.5 oz) chopped green chiles, well drained
- ½ cup shredded sharp Cheddar cheese (2 oz)
- ½ cup shredded hot pepper Monterey Jack cheese (2 oz)
- ¼ teaspoon garlic powder

1 Move oven rack to highest position. Heat oven to 375°F. Spray cookie sheet with cooking spray.

2 Do not unroll dough. Place dough on sprayed cookie sheet. Starting at center, press out dough to form 14×5-inch rectangle. Sprinkle chiles and cheeses evenly over dough to within 1/2 inch of long sides. Bring long sides up over cheese; pinch to seal. Pinch ends to seal. Sprinkle with garlic powder.

3 Bake 15 to 20 minutes or until golden brown. Cool 15 minutes. Cut into slices. Serve warm.

1 Serving: Calories 140; Total Fat 4.5g (Saturated Fat 2.5g; Trans Fat 0g); Cholesterol 10mg; Sodium 550mg; Total Carbohydrate 19g (Dietary Fiber 0g) • **Exchanges:** 1 Starch, ½ High-Fat Meat • **Carbohydrate Choices:** 1

Quick 'n Easy Herb Flatbread

Bake-Off® Contest 39, 2000   Cathy Olafson   Colorado Springs, CO

Prep Time: **10 Minutes**   Start to Finish: **25 Minutes**   9 servings

---

1 can (13.8 oz) Pillsbury refrigerated classic pizza crust

1 tablespoon olive or vegetable oil

½ to 1 teaspoon dried basil leaves

½ to 1 teaspoon dried rosemary leaves, crushed

½ teaspoon finely chopped garlic

⅛ teaspoon salt

1 small tomato

¼ cup shredded fresh Parmesan cheese

---

1 Heat oven to 425°F. Spray cookie sheet with cooking spray. Unroll dough; place on cookie sheet. Starting at center, press out dough to form 12×8-inch rectangle.

2 In small bowl, mix oil, basil, rosemary and garlic. Brush over dough; sprinkle with salt. Chop tomato; place in shallow bowl. With back of spoon, crush tomato. Spread tomato evenly over dough. Bake 5 to 9 minutes or until edges are light golden brown.

3 Sprinkle cheese evenly over partially baked crust. Bake 2 to 3 minutes longer or until and edges are golden brown and cheese is melted. Cut into squares. Serve warm.

---

1 Serving: Calories 140; Total Fat 3.5g (Saturated Fat 1g; Trans Fat 0g); Cholesterol 0mg; Sodium 400mg; Total Carbohydrate 21g (Dietary Fiber 0g) • **Exchanges:** 1 ½ Starch, ½ Fat • **Carbohydrate Choices:** 1 ½

Country French Herb Flatbread

Bake-Off® Contest 38, 1998   Leslie DiFiglio   St. Charles, IL

Prep Time: **15 Minutes**   Start to Finish: **35 Minutes**   20 servings

1 can (13.8 oz) Pillsbury refrigerated classic pizza crust	2 eggs
4 ½ teaspoons olive oil	Dash pepper
2 teaspoons herbes de Provence	Fresh thyme or rosemary sprigs, if desired
5 to 6 oil-packed sun-dried tomatoes, drained, chopped	Red and/or yellow cherry tomatoes, if desired
⅓ cup chèvre (goat) cheese, softened	

1 Heat oven to 400°F. Spray 13×9-inch pan with cooking spray. Unroll dough; place in pan. Starting at center, press out dough to edge of pan. With fingers, make indentations over surface of dough. Brush with 3 teaspoons of the oil. Sprinkle with 1 teaspoon of the herbes de Provence. Top with sun-dried tomatoes.

2 In medium bowl, mix cheese, eggs, remaining 1 1/2 teaspoons oil and remaining 1 teaspoon herbes de Provence, using wire whisk. Pour evenly over tomatoes; spread carefully.

3 Bake 15 to 20 minutes or until edges are golden brown. Sprinkle with pepper. If necessary, loosen sides of pizza from pan. Cut into squares.

1 Serving: Calories 80; Total Fat 3.5g (Saturated Fat 1.5g; Trans Fat 0g); Cholesterol 25mg; Sodium 170mg; Total Carbohydrate 10g (Dietary Fiber 0g) • **Exchanges:** ½ Starch, ½ High-Fat Meat • **Carbohydrate Choices:** ½

pizza bites To substitute the herbes de Provence, mix 1/2 teaspoon each dried thyme, marjoram, rosemary and basil leaves.

Sun-Dried Tomato and Olive Focaccia

Bake-Off® Contest 38, 1998   TerryAnn Moore   Oaklyn, NJ

Prep Time: **15 Minutes**   Start to Finish: **30 Minutes**   16 servings

1 can (13.8 oz) Pillsbury refrigerated classic pizza crust

¼ cup Caesar salad dressing

3 tablespoons finely chopped oil-packed sun-dried tomatoes, drained

3 tablespoons sliced ripe olives

3 tablespoons sliced pimiento-stuffed green olives

2 teaspoons chopped fresh or ½ teaspoon dried basil leaves

¾ cup chunky-style salsa, if desired

Fresh basil sprigs, if desired

1 Heat oven to 425°F. Lightly grease cookie sheet with shortening. Unroll dough; place on cookie sheet. Starting at center, press out dough to form 11×10-inch rectangle. Brush lightly with 3 tablespoons of the salad dressing. With fingers or handle of wooden spoon, make indentations in dough every 3 inches.

2 In small bowl, combine tomatoes, ripe and green olives, chopped basil and remaining salad dressing; mix well. Spoon mixture over crust; spread evenly.

3 Bake 8 to 12 minutes or until edges are golden brown. Cut into rectangles. Arrange on serving platter around bowl of salsa; garnish with basil sprigs.

1 Serving: Calories 90; Total Fat 3.5g (Saturated Fat 0.5g; Trans Fat 0g); Cholesterol 0mg; Sodium 260mg; Total Carbohydrate 12g (Dietary Fiber 0g) • **Exchanges:** ½ Starch, ½ Other Carbohydrate, ½ Fat • **Carbohydrate Choices:** 1

Speedy Spinach Squares Alfredo

Bake-Off® Contest 38, 1998   Debbie Powyszynski   Allen, TX

Prep Time: **10 Minutes**   Start to Finish: **30 Minutes**   8 servings

1 can (13.8 oz) Pillsbury refrigerated classic pizza crust

1 cup frozen cut leaf spinach

½ cup purchased Alfredo sauce

1 jar (4.5-oz) sliced mushrooms, well drained

2 cups shredded mozzarella cheese (8 oz)

4 ½ oz sliced cooked ham (½-inch thick), cut into 2×½-inch strips (1 cup)

⅓ cup chopped red bell pepper

Grated Parmesan cheese, if desired

Crushed red pepper flakes, if desired

1   Heat oven to 425°F. Lightly grease 13×9-inch (3-quart) baking dish with shortening. Unroll dough; place in pan. Starting at center, press out dough to edge of pan and halfway up sides.

2   Place spinach in small microwave-safe bowl. Cover; microwave on High for 2 minutes. Drain well; squeeze out moisture. Pat dry with paper towel.

3   Spoon and spread Alfredo sauce evenly over dough. Arrange spinach over sauce; press slightly. Top with mushrooms, mozzarella cheese, ham and bell pepper.

4   Bake 15 to 17 minutes or until crust is golden brown. Cut into squares. Sprinkle with Parmesan cheese and red pepper flakes.

1 Serving: Calories 300; Total Fat 13g (Saturated Fat 7g; Trans Fat 0g); Cholesterol 40mg; Sodium 880mg; Total Carbohydrate 27g (Dietary Fiber 1g) • **Exchanges:** 1 Starch, 1 Other Carbohydrate, 2 Lean Meat, 1 Fat • **Carbohydrate Choices:** 2

Antipasto Appetizer Pizza

Bake-Off® Contest 41, 2004   Brandy Koproski   Oswego, NY

Prep Time: 20 Minutes   Start to Finish: **40 Minutes**   16 servings

1 ½ teaspoons all-purpose flour

1 can (13.8 oz) Pillsbury refrigerated classic pizza crust

1 jar (7 to 7.25 oz) roasted red bell peppers, drained, chopped

1 jar (6 to 7 oz) marinated artichoke hearts, drained, chopped

¾ cup drained pitted ripe olives, chopped

3 oz thinly sliced Genoa salami, cut into ½-inch pieces

3 oz thinly sliced provolone cheese, cut into ½-inch pieces (¾ cup)

4 oz feta cheese, crumbled (1 cup)

½ teaspoon dried Italian seasoning, if desired

1 Heat oven to 400°F. Sprinkle flour evenly over cookie sheet. Unroll dough; place on cookie sheet. Starting at center, press out dough to form 14×10-inch rectangle.

2 Sprinkle roasted peppers, artichokes and olives evenly over dough. Top with salami, provolone cheese and feta cheese. Sprinkle with Italian seasoning.

3 Bake 15 to 20 minutes or until edge of crust is golden brown and cheese is melted. Cut into squares. Serve warm.

1 Serving: Calories 140; Total Fat 6g (Saturated Fat 3g; Trans Fat 0g); Cholesterol 15mg; Sodium 490mg; Total Carbohydrate 15g (Dietary Fiber 0g) • **Exchanges:** ½ Starch, ½ Other Carbohydrate, ½ High-Fat Meat, ½ Fat • **Carbohydrate Choices:** 1

pizza bites Try Kalamata olives instead of ripe olives. These Greek olives are a dark eggplant color with a rich and fruity flavor. Look for already-pitted Kalamata olives to save a little time.

Pizza Squares Continental

Bake-Off® Contest 38, 1998   Gilda Lester   Wilmington, NC

Prep Time: **30 Minutes**   Start to Finish: **55 Minutes**   16 servings

2 tablespoons olive oil

2 large onions, thinly sliced (4 cups)

1 can (13.8 oz) Pillsbury refrigerated classic pizza crust

6 oz sliced provolone cheese

1 jar (7 to 7.25 oz) roasted red bell peppers, drained, cut into thin strips

2 oz Montrachet or other chèvre (goat) cheese, crumbled (⅓ cup)

2 tablespoons pine nuts, if desired

1 Heat oven to 425°F. Grease 12-inch pizza pan or 13×9-inch pan with shortening. Heat oil in large skillet over medium heat until hot. Add onions; cook 10 to 12 minutes or until light golden brown, stirring occasionally.

2 Meanwhile, unroll dough; place in pan. Starting at center, press out dough to edge of pan. Arrange provolone cheese over dough. Spoon onions over cheese. Top with roasted bell peppers and Montrachet cheese.

3 Bake 16 to 21 minutes or until crust is golden brown. Sprinkle with pine nuts. Cut into wedges or squares.

1 Serving: Calories 140; Total Fat 6g (Saturated Fat 3g; Trans Fat 0g); Cholesterol 10mg; Sodium 290mg; Total Carbohydrate 16g (Dietary Fiber 0g) • **Exchanges:** 1 Starch, ½ High-Fat Meat • **Carbohydrate Choices:** 1

Wild Mushroom Pizza

Prep Time: **15 Minutes**   Start to Finish: **35 Minutes**   48 servings

1 teaspoon olive oil

1 can (13.8 oz) Pillsbury refrigerated classic pizza crust

1 tablespoon butter or margarine

1 lb assorted fresh wild mushrooms (shiitake, oyster, crimini), cut into ¼-inch-thick slices

1 teaspoon dried thyme leaves, crushed

Salt and pepper, if desired

1 package (8 oz) ⅓-less-fat cream cheese (Neufchâtel), softened

4 oz fontina cheese, shredded (1 cup)

1 cup shredded mozzarella cheese (4 oz)

1 Heat oven to 400°F. Brush large cookie sheet with olive oil. Unroll dough; place on cookie sheet. Starting at center, press out dough into 15×10-inch rectangle. Bake 8 to 10 minutes or until crust is very light brown.

2 Meanwhile, in 12-inch skillet, heat butter over medium-high heat until melted. Add mushrooms; cook about 6 minutes, stirring frequently, until well browned; drain. Stir in thyme, salt and pepper.

3 Spread cream cheese evenly over partially baked crust. Sprinkle fontina cheese over cream cheese. Spread cooked mushrooms over cheese. Sprinkle mozzarella cheese over mushrooms.

4 Bake 10 to 12 minutes longer or until crust is golden brown and cheese is melted. Cool 5 minutes. Cut into 8 rows by 6 rows.

1 Serving: Calories 50; Total Fat 3g (Saturated Fat 1.5g; Trans Fat 0g); Cholesterol 10mg; Sodium 110mg; Total Carbohydrate 4g (Dietary Fiber 0g) • **Exchanges:** ½ High-Fat Meat • **Carbohydrate Choices:** 0

pizza bites Fontina has a sharp, yet delicate piquant flavor. Gruyere, provolone, Gouda or Edam are also tasty on this pizza.

Spicy Provolone Cheese Pizza

Bake-Off® Contest 34, 1990   Gilda Lester   Chadds Ford, PA

Prep Time: **20 Minutes**   Start to Finish: **35 Minutes**   24 servings

1 can (13.8 oz) Pillsbury refrigerated classic pizza crust

2 to 4 tablespoons olive oil

1 large onion, finely chopped (1 cup)

3 cloves garlic, finely chopped

½ teaspoon dried oregano leaves

½ teaspoon dried basil leaves

½ teaspoon dried parsley flakes

½ teaspoon dried thyme leaves

¼ to ½ teaspoon crushed red pepper flakes

8 oz sliced provolone cheese

¼ cup sliced ripe olives, drained

1 Heat oven to 425°F. Lightly grease large cookie sheet or 15×10-inch pan with shortening. Unroll dough; place on cookie sheet. Starting at center, press out dough to form 15×10-inch rectangle. Form 1/4-inch rim around edges.

2 In 8-inch skillet, heat oil over medium-high heat until hot. Cook onion and garlic in oil about 5 minutes, stirring frequently, until lightly browned. Stir in oregano, basil, parsley, thyme and pepper flakes.

3 Spoon onion mixture evenly over dough. Arrange cheese slices over onions. Sprinkle with olives.

4 Bake 9 to 13 minutes or until crust is golden brown and cheese is melted. Cut into squares.

1 Serving: Calories 90; Total Fat 4.5g (Saturated Fat 2g; Trans Fat 0g); Cholesterol 5mg; Sodium 210mg; Total Carbohydrate 9g (Dietary Fiber 0g) • **Exchanges:** ½ Starch, ½ High-Fat Meat • **Carbohydrate Choices:** ½

pizza bites No time to chop garlic? Use 1 1/2 teaspoons purchased chopped garlic or 3/8 teaspoon garlic powder.

Easy Vegetable Pizza

Prep Time: **20 Minutes**   Start to Finish: **1 Hour 10 Minutes**   32 appetizers

2 cans (8 oz each) Pillsbury refrigerated crescent dinner rolls

1 package (8 oz) cream cheese, softened

½ cup sour cream

1 teaspoon dried dill weed

⅛ teaspoon garlic powder

½ cup small fresh broccoli florets

⅓ cup quartered cucumber slices

1 plum (Roma) tomato, seeded, chopped

¼ cup shredded carrot

¼ cup finely chopped yellow bell pepper

1 Heat oven to 375°F. Separate cans of dough into 4 long rectangles. In ungreased 15×10-inch pan, place dough; press in bottom and up sides to form crust. Bake 13 to 17 minutes or until golden brown. Cool completely, about 30 minutes.

2 Meanwhile, in small bowl, mix cream cheese, sour cream, dill and garlic powder until smooth.

3 Spread cream cheese mixture evenly over baked and cooled crust. Top with vegetables. Serve immediately, or cover and refrigerate 1 to 2 hours before serving. Cut into 16 squares; cut each square in half diagonally or cut into 32 squares.

1 Appetizer: Calories 90; Total Fat 6g (Saturated Fat 3g; Trans Fat 1g); Cholesterol 10mg; Sodium 135mg; Total Carbohydrate 6g (Dietary Fiber 0g) • **Exchanges:** ½ Starch • **Carbohydrate Choices:** ½

pizza bites For the best results, keep the crescent roll dough in the refrigerator until you're ready to use it. Cold dough bakes the best!

Brie and Cranberry Pizza

Bake-Off® Contest 38, 1998   Didi Fraioli   Huntington, NY

Prep Time: **10 Minutes**   Start to Finish: **35 Minutes**   16 appetizers

1 can (8 oz) Pillsbury refrigerated crescent dinner rolls

1 package (8 oz) Brie cheese, rind removed, cut into ½-inch cubes

¾ cup canned whole berry cranberry sauce

½ cup chopped pecans

1 Heat oven to 425°F. Lightly oil 12-inch pizza pan or 13×9-inch pan with olive or vegetable oil. Unroll dough; separate into triangles. Place triangles in oiled pan with tips toward center. Press out dough. Bake 5 to 8 minutes or until light golden brown.

2 Sprinkle cheese over partially baked crust. Place cranberry sauce in small bowl; stir to break up pieces. Spoon cranberry sauce by teaspoonfuls evenly over cheese. Sprinkle with pecans.

3 Bake 6 to 10 minutes longer or crust is golden brown and cheese is melted. Cool 5 minutes. Cut into wedges or squares.

1 Appetizer: Calories 150; Total Fat 9g (Saturated Fat 3.5g; Trans Fat 1g); Cholesterol 15mg; Sodium 200mg; Total Carbohydrate 11g (Dietary Fiber 0g) • **Exchanges:** ½ Starch, ½ High-Fat Meat, 1 Fat • **Carbohydrate Choices:** 1

Fanciful Fruit Pizza

Prep Time: **20 Minutes**   Start to Finish: **2 Hours 10 Minutes**   12 servings

1 roll (16.5 oz) Pillsbury Create 'n Bake™ refrigerated sugar cookies

1 package (8 oz) cream cheese, softened

⅓ cup sugar

½ teaspoon vanilla

1 cup fresh or canned peach slices, drained, cut into thinner slices

1 cup halved or quartered fresh strawberries

1 cup fresh or frozen blueberries

½ cup apple jelly

1 Heat oven to 350°F. Grease 12-inch pizza pan with shortening or spray with cooking spray. In pan, break up cookie dough into pieces; press out evenly to form crust. Bake 16 to 20 minutes or until golden brown. Cool completely, about 30 minutes.

2 Meanwhile, in small bowl, beat cream cheese, sugar and vanilla with electric mixer on medium speed until fluffy. Spread mixture over cooled crust. Arrange fruit over cream cheese.

3 Stir jelly until smooth; spoon or brush over fruit. Refrigerate until chilled, at least 1 hour. Cut into wedges or squares to serve. Cover and refrigerate any remaining pizza.

1 Serving: Calories 320; Total Fat 15g (Saturated Fat 6g; Trans Fat 2g); Cholesterol 35mg; Sodium 170mg; Total Carbohydrate 43g (Dietary Fiber 0g) • **Exchanges:** 3 Other Carbohydrate, ½ High-Fat Meat, 2 Fat • **Carbohydrate Choices:** 3

pizza bites For a winter fruit pizza, use 1 cup fresh or canned pear slices, drained, cut into thinner slices, 1 cup mandarin orange segments, drained, and 2 kiwifruit, peeled and sliced.

Fruity Almond Dessert Pizza

Bake-Off® Contest 38, 1998   Rosemary Leicht   Bethel, OH

Prep Time: **15 Minutes**   Start to Finish: **45 Minutes**   8 servings

1 can (13.8 oz) Pillsbury refrigerated classic pizza crust

⅓ cup cream cheese or light cream cheese, softened

¼ cup apricot preserves

1 large apple, peeled, thinly sliced

¼ cup all-purpose or unbleached flour

¼ cup packed brown sugar

2 tablespoons butter or margarine

¼ cup blanched almonds, coarsely chopped

1 Heat oven to 425°F. Grease 12-inch pizza pan or 13×9-inch pan with shortening, or spray with cooking spray. Unroll dough; place in pan. Starting at center, press out dough to edge of pan. Spread cream cheese evenly over dough. Spread with preserves. Arrange apple slices over preserves.

2 In small bowl, mix flour and brown sugar. With pastry blender or fork, cut in butter until mixture resembles coarse crumbs. Stir in almonds. Sprinkle mixture evenly over apples.

3 Bake 15 to 20 minutes or until edges are golden brown. Cool 10 minutes. Cut into wedges. Serve warm.

1 Serving: Calories 290; Total Fat 10g (Saturated Fat 4.5g; Trans Fat 0g); Cholesterol 20mg; Sodium 410mg; Total Carbohydrate 44g (Dietary Fiber 0g) • **Exchanges:** 1 Starch, 2 Other Carbohydrate, ½ High-Fat Meat, 1 Fat • **Carbohydrate Choices:** 3

Apple Streusel Pizzas

Prep Time: **15 Minutes**   Start to Finish: **30 Minutes**   4 pizzas

1 can (13.8 oz) Pillsbury
refrigerated classic pizza crust

2 large Braeburn apples,
peeled, thinly sliced
(2 ½ cups)

¼ cup wheat germ

3 tablespoons brown sugar

1 tablespoon all-purpose or
unbleached flour

½ teaspoon ground cinnamon

2 tablespoons butter, melted

1 Heat oven to 425°F. Spray large cookie sheet with cooking spray.
Unroll dough; cut into 4 rectangles. Place on cookie sheet. Divide
apple slices evenly onto dough rectangles; press apples firmly into
dough.

2 In small bowl, combine all remaining ingredients; mix well. Sprinkle
about 2 tablespoons streusel mixture evenly over apples on each
rectangle.

3 Bake 10 to 13 minutes or until edges of crust are deep golden brown.
Serve warm.

1 Pizza: Calories 420; Total Fat 10g (Saturated Fat 4.5g; Trans Fat 0g); Cholesterol 15mg;
Sodium 750mg; Total Carbohydrate 74g (Dietary Fiber 2g) • **Exchanges:** 2 ½ Starch, 2 ½
Other Carbohydrate, 1 ½ Fat • **Carbohydrate Choices:** 5

pizza bites New Zealand's crisp, sweet Braeburn apples have
become a favorite. Substitute your apple of choice if you can't find
Braeburns.

Banana Split–Brownie Pizza

Prep Time: **20 Minutes**   Start to Finish: **1 Hour 40 Minutes**   16 servings

1 roll (16.5 oz) Pillsbury
refrigerated traditional
chocolate fudge brownies

1 package (8 oz) cream
cheese, softened

1 can (8 oz) crushed pineapple,
drained

2 bananas, sliced

1 cup sliced fresh strawberries

¼ cup chocolate topping

1   Heat oven to 350°F. Line 12×3/4-inch pizza pan with foil; grease and flour foil. Spread brownie batter on foil in pan.

2   Bake 15 to 18 minutes or until toothpick inserted near center comes out clean. Cool completely, about 1 hour.

3   Meanwhile, in small bowl, beat cream cheese and pineapple on low speed until blended. Spread over brownie; top with fruit. Drizzle chocolate topping over fruit. Refrigerate until serving time. Cut into 16 wedges or squares. Cover and refrigerate any remaining pizza.

1 Serving: Calories 210; Total Fat 10g (Saturated Fat 4g; Trans Fat 1.5g); Cholesterol 15mg; Sodium 135mg; Total Carbohydrate 28g (Dietary Fiber 0g) • **Exchanges:** 2 Other Carbohydrate, ½ High-Fat Meat, 1 Fat • **Carbohydrate Choices:** 2

pizza bites If the chocolate topping is too thick to drizzle, microwave as directed on the container.

Mini Fruit Pizzas

Prep Time: **40 Minutes**   Start to Finish: **40 Minutes**   20 fruit pizzas

1 package (18 oz) Pillsbury Ready to Bake!® refrigerated sugar cookies

1 package (8 oz) cream cheese, softened

2 tablespoons frozen limeade concentrate, thawed

½ cup powdered sugar

10 fresh strawberries, quartered

1 kiwifruit, peeled, halved lengthwise and cut into 10 slices

½ cup fresh blueberries

½ cup fresh raspberries

1 Heat oven to 350°F. Bake cookies as directed on package. Cool completely, about 10 minutes.

2 Meanwhile, in medium bowl, beat cream cheese, limeade concentrate and powdered sugar until smooth.

3 Spread each cookie with 1 tablespoon cream cheese mixture. Arrange fruit on top of each. Serve immediately, or cover and refrigerate up to 2 hours.

1 Fruit Pizza: Calories 180; Total Fat 10g (Saturated Fat 4.5g; Trans Fat 2g); Cholesterol 20mg; Sodium 100mg; Total Carbohydrate 21g (Dietary Fiber 0g) • **Exchanges:** ½ Starch, 1 Other Carbohydrate, 2 Fat • **Carbohydrate Choices:** 1 ½

Rocky Road Cookie Pizza

Prep Time: **20 Minutes**   Start to Finish: **1 Hour 55 Minutes**   16 servings

1 roll (16.5 oz) Pillsbury Create 'n Bake refrigerated double chocolate chip & chunk or chocolate chip cookies

1 cup miniature marshmallows

½ cup salted peanuts

½ cup semisweet chocolate chips

⅓ cup caramel topping

1 Heat oven to 350°F. Grease 12-inch pizza pan with shortening, or spray with cooking spray. In pan, break up cookie dough into pieces and press out dough evenly in bottom of pan to form crust. Bake 12 to 17 minutes or until light golden brown.

2 Sprinkle marshmallows, peanuts and chocolate chips evenly over partially baked crust. Drizzle with caramel topping.

3 Bake 8 to 10 minutes longer or until topping is melted. Cool completely, about 1 hour 15 minutes. Cut into wedges to serve.

1 Serving: Calories 210; Total Fat 9g (Saturated Fat 3g; Trans Fat 1g); Cholesterol 5mg; Sodium 130mg; Total Carbohydrate 29g (Dietary Fiber 0g) • **Exchanges:** 2 Other Carbohydrate, ½ High-Fat Meat, 1 Fat • **Carbohydrate Choices:** 2

pizza bites You could use milk chocolate chips or white vanilla baking chips instead of the semisweet chips.

Chocolate–Peanut Butter Cookie Pizza

Prep Time: **15 Minutes** Start to Finish: **1 Hour 30 Minutes**   12 servings

1 roll (16.5 oz) Pillsbury
Create 'n Bake refrigerated
chocolate chip cookies

1 package (8 oz) cream
cheese, softened

½ cup creamy peanut butter

1 cup powdered sugar

¼ cup milk

1 cup frozen whipped topping,
thawed

¾ cup hot fudge topping

¼ cup chopped peanuts

1 Heat oven to 350°F. In ungreased 12-inch pizza pan, break up cookie
dough into pieces. With floured fingers, press out dough evenly in
bottom of pan to form crust. Bake 15 to 20 minutes or until golden
brown. Cool completely, about 30 minutes.

2 Meanwhile, in medium bowl, beat cream cheese, peanut butter,
powdered sugar and milk until smooth. Fold in whipped topping.

3 Spread 1/2 cup of the fudge topping over cooled crust. Spread
peanut butter mixture over top. Drizzle with remaining 1/4 cup fudge
topping. Sprinkle with peanuts. Refrigerate at least 30 minutes or until
serving time. Cut into wedges or squares.

1 Serving: Calories 440; Total Fat 23g (Saturated Fat 9g; Trans Fat 1.5g); Cholesterol
30mg; Sodium 300mg; Total Carbohydrate 51g (Dietary Fiber 1g) • **Exchanges:** 3 ½
Other Carbohydrate, 1 High-Fat Meat, 3 Fat • **Carbohydrate Choices:** 3 ½

pizza bites Prepare the cookie pizza crust up to a day ahead of time.
After it's cooled, wrap it tightly in plastic wrap and store at room temperature
until you're ready to top it off.

Helpful Nutrition and Cooking Information

Nutrition Guidelines

We provide nutrition information for each recipe—that includes calories, fat, cholesterol, sodium, carbohydrate and fiber. Individual food choices can be based on this information.

Recommended intake for a daily diet of 2,000 calories as set by the Food and Drug Administration

Total Fat	Less than 65g
Saturated Fat	Less than 20g
Cholesterol	Less than 300mg
Sodium	Less than 2,400mg
Total Carbohydrate	300g
Dietary Fiber	25g

Criteria Used for Calculating Nutrition Information

- The first ingredient is used wherever a choice is given (such as ⅓ cup sour cream or plain yogurt).

- The first ingredient amount was used wherever a range is given (such as 3- to 3-½–pound cut-up broiler-fryer chicken).

- The first serving number was used wherever a range is given (such as 4 to 6 servings).

- "If desired" ingredients and recipe variations were not included (such as sprinkle with brown sugar, if desired).

- Only the amount of a marinade or frying oil that is estimated to be absorbed by the food during preparation or cooking was calculated.

Ingredients Used in Recipe Testing and Nutrition Calculations

- Ingredients used for testing represent those that the majority of consumers use in their homes: large eggs, 2% milk, 80%-lean ground beef and canned ready-to-use chicken broth.

- Fat-free, low-fat or low-sodium products were not used, unless otherwise indicated.

- Solid vegetable shortening was used to grease pans, unless otherwise indicated.

Equipment Used in Recipe Testing

We use equipment for testing that the majority of consumers use in their homes. If a specific piece of equipment (such as a wire whisk) is necessary for recipe success, it is listed in the recipe.

- Cookware and bakeware without nonstick coatings were used, unless otherwise indicated.

- No dark-colored, black or insulated bakeware was used.

- When a pan is specified in a recipe, a metal pan was used; a baking dish or pie plate means ovenproof glass was used.

- An electric hand mixer was used for mixing only when mixer speeds are specified in the recipe directions. When a mixer speed is not given, a spoon or fork was used.

Cooking Terms Glossary

Beat: Mix ingredients vigorously with spoon, fork, wire whisk, hand beater or electric mixer until smooth and uniform.

Boil: Heat liquid until bubbles rise continuously and break on the surface and steam is given off. For rolling boil, the bubbles form rapidly.

Chop: Cut into coarse or fine irregular pieces with a knife, food chopper, blender or food processor.

Cube: Cut into squares ½ inch or larger.

Dice: Cut into squares smaller than ½ inch.

Grate: Cut into tiny particles using small rough holes of grater (citrus peel or chocolate).

Grease: Rub the inside surface of a pan with shortening, using pastry brush, piece of waxed paper or paper towel, to prevent food from sticking during baking (as for some casseroles).

Julienne: Cut into thin, matchlike strips, using knife or food processor (vegetables, fruits, meats).

Mix: Combine ingredients in any way that distributes them evenly.

Sauté: Cook foods in hot oil or margarine over medium-high heat with frequent tossing and turning motion.

Shred: Cut into long thin pieces by rubbing food across the holes of a shredder, as for cheese, or by using a knife to slice very thinly, as for cabbage.

Simmer: Cook in liquid just below the boiling point on top of the stove; usually after reducing heat from a boil. Bubbles will rise slowly and break just below the surface.

Stir: Mix ingredients until uniform consistency. Stir once in a while for stirring occasionally, often for stirring frequently and continuously for stirring constantly.

Toss: Tumble ingredients (such as green salad) lightly with a lifting motion, usually to coat evenly or mix with another food.

Metric Conversion Guide

VOLUME

U.S. Units	Canadian Metric	Australian Metric
¼ teaspoon	1 mL	1 ml
½ teaspoon	2 mL	2 ml
1 teaspoon	5 mL	5 ml
1 tablespoon	15 mL	20 ml
¼ cup	50 mL	60 ml
⅓ cup	75 mL	80 ml
½ cup	125 mL	125 ml
⅔ cup	150 mL	170 ml
¾ cup	175 mL	190 ml
1 cup	250 mL	250 ml
1 quart	1 liter	1 liter
1 ½ quarts	1.5 liters	1.5 liters
2 quarts	2 liters	2 liters
2 ½ quarts	2.5 liters	2.5 liters
3 quarts	3 liters	3 liters
4 quarts	4 liters	4 liters

WEIGHT

U.S. Units	Canadian Metric	Australian Metric
1 ounce	30 grams	30 grams
2 ounces	55 grams	60 grams
3 ounces	85 grams	90 grams
4 ounces (¼ pound)	115 grams	125 grams
8 ounces (½ pound)	225 grams	225 grams
16 ounces (1 pound)	455 grams	500 grams
1 pound	455 grams	½ kilogram

MEASUREMENTS

Inches	Centimeters
1	2.5
2	5.0
3	7.5
4	10.0
5	12.5
6	15.0
7	17.5
8	20.5
9	23.0
10	25.5
11	28.0
12	30.5
13	33.0

TEMPERATURES

Fahrenheit	Celsius
32°	0°
212°	100°
250°	120°
275°	140°
300°	150°
325°	160°
350°	180°
375°	190°
400°	200°
425°	220°
450°	230°
475°	240°
500°	260°

NOTE: The recipes in this cookbook have not been developed or tested using metric measures. When converting recipes to metric, some variations in quality may be noted.

Index

Page numbers in *italics* indicate illustrations.

Whatever's on the menu,
make it easy with Pillsbury

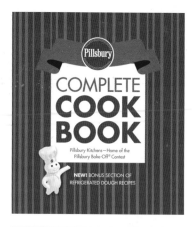

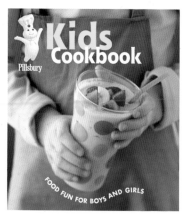

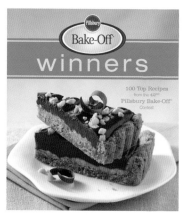